READER REVIEWS…

…provided a very real account of how someone with Asperger's operates in the world, in terms of being left out, often misunderstood, and not being able to pick up the social cues that serves to engage and protect people.

Tara Odovichuc, Life Coach

This could be a sad story but in Margaret Adam's skillful storytelling hands, it is an elating story. We viscerally experience a girl who is emotionally curious and refreshingly candid (to the point of startling honesty); an unforgettable girl who refuses to collapse in on herself.

Betsy Warland, author of *Breathing the Page – Reading the Act of Writing*

UNFORGIVING
The Memoir of An Asperger Teen

by

Margaret Jean Adam

JERVIS DISTRIBUTORS, VANCOUVER, BC

This book gives voice to the ways in which a child is made vulnerable because of somehow missing that all-important developmental connection to family. It is meant to speak without pity or affectation to one child's cry for help and to acknowledge with dignity and outrage the power and limitations of a child determined to help herself.

In this volume, I offer my readers a glimpse into a difficult time in my youth. Persons' names have been changed due to the discussion of sexual predators in of parts of this book, and to protect people who may not wish to be associated with such a history. Place names have not been changed. My name is unchanged.

Knowing full well that some subjects are seldom spoken of due to a polite reserve, I have broached them in the hope that parents and others may have a better understanding of how these things occur.

National Library of Canada cataloguing in publication

Adam, Margaret Jean
Unforgiving, The Memoir of an Asperger Teen

ISBN: 0973136421
ISBN-13: 9780973136425

Published by Jervis Distributors.

Editing & Formatting: Coast Editing Services.
Cover Design: James Findlay.
Cover Photo: Unknown.

ACKNOWLEDGEMENTS

For uncompromising faith in my ability, being my biggest fan, and my best husband, Chris Florczak.

From Simon Fraser University:
Roy Miki for his last class at SFU which inspired this project.

Betsy Warland's editing suggestions, invaluable in the rethink of certain portions of the manuscript.

Fred Wah early in the project for his input.

Jeff Derksen for encouraging me from day one, for putting my poem on his Third Year BC Lit syllabus and generally making me feel competent in the area of the English language.

The readerly input and insights of my daughter, Beverly, and my friend, Care Hanna, and my Belmont ex-pat, Marilyn Pitman.

To Tara Odovichuc for reading this manuscript through the lens of seven years of counseling sex offenders.

Colin Sprake and The BEST group especially Richard Hutton, the above-mentioned Care Hanna, and Marishu Fehr. From Triple Win, the buoyant and loyal Chris Nelmes, Harmony Thiessen, and Jason Nitroman.

To Kasia Rachsfall, who was always there when I needed her.

To my sister, Myra, who is my anchor, and my sister-in-law, Kamla, who believes.

Our lives begin to end the day we become silent about things that matter.

Martin Luther King

CHAPTER 1

See that chair my Grandmother, Mrs. Esme Adam, is sitting in? It was big and soft and brown, and positioned just right so that the sun from the windows beamed down on me while I read. And if the house was empty, (oh rare occasion!) I might fall asleep, a book open on my lap.

I had a dream in that chair, a dream that I was in the forest, hotly pursued by fiercely painted, tomahawk-wielding, war-whooping Indians. My heart slammed against my chest as I ran, my legs felt like lead and sweat streamed down my forehead.

I was terribly, horribly alone on a wide plain with no help in sight. And then I saw a cliff edge and a gigantic log that seemed to reach another side. I dashed up it, only to find it hovering over a ravine so deep it gaped endless beneath me. Balanced precariously, I lurched to a halt as the log suddenly ended. My heart beat louder than native tom-toms as I wobbled uncertainly on the brink of a dark abyss.

By now my pursuers were so close I could smell the sweat beading on their faces, and see the chiselled edges of their tomahawks.

There was only me and I was only eleven, and I had to do something or die. I did not call for my mother or father. Instead I said, "This is *my* dream, okay? So we're going to say that I went this way, and you went that way."

And to my astonishment, they did.

CHAPTER 2

Diary: Mrs. Esme Adam.
Friday, July 12, 1963

    Edna's last day at laundry. Busy. Tommy mowed grass & tidied for hours. Marg vacuumed & made shortcake for supper. Maria[1] here for supper & evening, & Canasta card games.

July 16, 1963

    Edna and I watered garden, etc. Tommy sold truck & they painted Marg and Terry's room.

    Marg picked 15 lbs. raspberries at Scotneys. I fixed jars and fruit and Edna processed.

    Tommy to Duncan to AA.

My grandmother doesn't elaborate on what *Edna's last day at laundry* means. Perhaps my father, Tommy, having newly found sobriety, wanted her to quit to make up for some of the wrong he'd done her. Perhaps it was just a brief break before the annual trip to the prairies with the younger kids, my sister, Terry, who is eight[2] and my younger brother, Scott who is five. Or maybe my mother, Edna, suffering from migraines, depression and back problems, just quit.

How calm and industrious our recounted life: "Busy". Our grandmother dutifully notes our guest, Maria, at dinner, partaking of the bread my mother baked. Staying for a card game after. What innocent fun it all sounds.

There is no mention of the cleavage that rose and fell with Maria's throaty laugh, the cruel slash of carmine lipstick that left corrugated lip prints on our green glassware mugs. Or how she would pucker up those vivid lips in a threat to kiss Scotty, sending him shrieking down the hall or scurrying under the table.

Perhaps there are not enough lines to describe the way she lit one cigarette with the sizzling tip of another, her dancing eyes squinting at my father through the smoke as she inhaled, expanding those mountainous bosoms.

Nor does my grandmother describe my mother, her translucent skin grey with the exhaustion of working in the moist heat of the Empress Hotel laundry all day, her faded housedress in need of mending, her blue eyes sad and slightly amused, mere ashes of a woman sitting across from the incendiary Maria.

You would think that I would feel some sympathy for my mother, a pale, weary woman suffering in comparison to a lusty virago like Maria. But I did not. My heart was closed to my mother with all the resoluteness that only the young can summon and maintain. She had said what she said to me, words never explored or explained, so they remained, a barrier more severe and impenetrable than any vault door. I, the unforgiven, would in turn, refuse to forgive.

And so she was simply nothing to me. A powerless person to be observed, a fellow traveler with whom one is inadvertently billeted and with whom certain proprieties must be observed, certain acknowledgements made in passing, ritual phrases uttered without thought or care—except to preserve appearances.

I was sixteen, and I knew I was motherless in spite of that feminine creature that shared my father's bed, and gave her life to menial outside work and in between, managed what remnants of our lives we allotted her.

Maria would accompany my father to the Alcoholics Anonymous meetings. Grams didn't mention that, either, or how quiet the house was at three a.m. when he quietly turned his key in the lock. He would slip in, taking great care in closing the door, removing his shoes, and creeping down the hallway into bed.

Wed. July 17, 1963.

Edna made up bread and did the wash, and to town with Tommy on business. Marg & I baked off the bread & she ironed a bit and washed jars sterilized & filled 17 quarts raspberries & Edna canned. Luke[3] wrote Tommy; Floyd in poor shape[4].

At sixteen, I knew I did not want to become my mother. In fact, I was terrified of becoming my mother. Caught in a power dynamic between my self-centered, strong-willed father and an equally stubborn mother-in-law, Mom had the further indignity of putting up with Dad's women.

He always had affairs with women in our limited social circle, which must have made it an even worse hell for Mom. I watched her go out to work at seven o'clock in the morning, come home exhausted at five or six o'clock at night, and on her days off, do laundry for all us kids, Dad and my grandmother, bake a week's supply of buns, loaves and cinnamon rolls, do the ironing, cooking and what cleaning she had energy for.

And then Dad would always want her to go out Saturday night. I realize now what I couldn't see then—that she was too tired to deal with him or anything else in her life. Bone weary. That was Mom.

I didn't want to be like that! I wanted to be glamorous. Exciting. Busy. Have pretty clothes, and make-up and lots of friends and wonderful things going on all the time. Like an actress, a writer, a songwriter. A wife? No way. A mother? Not in my cards. I was going to be a star.

At the age of sixteen, I'd won a trophy for drama in high school, and honorable mention in a provincial drama competition. It didn't bother me that academically I was all over the place. I got straight A's in English, B's in French and failed Math, Science and Socials. All the same, my essay on the deterioration of the character of MacBeth (13 pages), was put in the school library in the research section. So regardless of the fact that I was going to have a lot of trouble graduating from high school, I saw myself as an up and comer.

In the meantime, we gardened and baked, preserved and kept house, Grandma and Mom talking briefly about Floyd's cancer while shelling peas or "putting up" fruit in sterile jars, the purple blood of blackberries staining our hands and aprons.

Thurs. July 18, 1963

Steve[5] phoned Edna and Tommy at 3 A.M. that Floyd, our darling, had passed away at Rose Valley Hospital. Edna, Tommy & Scott left for the 2 PM boat. Kenny[6] to bring Terry[7] to Lilloet to meet them. Nell[8] phoned Edna & Tommy.

Diary: Margaret Jean Adam: Sixteen Years Old.
July 20, 1963. Sunday.
Dear Diary,

Guess what? I'm home alone! Well, almost. Mom and Dad and the kids have gone to Saskatchewan[a] for Uncle Floyd's funeral. I got to stay home to look after Grams.

Poor Grams; Uncle Floyd's her oldest, Dad's big brother. I didn't know him much 'cause they live zillions of miles from here in a flat, dusty old place called Saskatchewan. Mom and Dad and Grams and all the aunts and uncles talk a lot about the prairies, using words like "home". Which I don't really get, because I mean, they all packed up and moved out here, didn't they? I might be failing geography but I do know that this

---

a Saskatchewan: A central Canadian prairie province, home to Floyd and birthplace of Edna and Matt and Margaret Jean.

island is as far west as you can get from the old farm. Anyway, Uncle Floyd's passing, which happened a few days ago, hit Grams pretty hard, what with Grampa dying a few years back, and Uncle Floyd being her oldest, and all. Although, if you ask me, Dad is totally her favorite. I mean, she's lived with us, like forever.

Anyway, you can't believe what I saw in the paper today. A film is being made in town, and they want teen-age girls to try out for the lead role. Dad would never let me do this in a trillion gazillion years, but he isn't here and even though Grams will fink me out as soon as they get back, by then, it's gonna be TOO LATE. I'll get lectured on hell and the devil and the pitfalls of Hollywood. Maybe I'll get the strap, too. But hey, I'm going! And I don't even have to ask, just tell Grams, because with Grams, anything "artistic" is okay.

Yours truly,
Margaret Jean

CHAPTER 3

Tues. July 23, 1963

Marg took 9:15 bus to go for Drama tests. Back on 12:30. She washed floor in boy's room. I went to bank & borrowed 25.00 for the insurances ($13.38) and expenses. To Cooper's Store. Nicky took Marg out.

Bumping along in the Langford bus on my way to the audition, I feel excitement shimmering like molten joy in my veins. *It doesn't matter if I don't get the part*, I tell myself, not even if they send me home and I bus my way back into my old bread-baking, sheet-changing, house-cleaning way of life. All that really counts is being gutsy enough to open a door to a totally different kind of life, not just peer in through a crack, but walk right up to the desk, give my name and say, "I'm here to try out for the film". No excuses, like *Dad will kill me when he gets back*, or *I have nothing to wear*! Not one.

❖ ❖ ❖

On that July morning, I awoke accepting for myself all the possibilities available in life, open to all the wonders my Margaret Jeanness could embrace, and I carried that openness, that power of possibilities down our long pot-holed dirt and gravel driveway, up Station Road, and onto the little path that led across the tracks, past where the ashes still lay black against the dusty red earth where the ties had burned that day last summer.

Walking past the ashes, I remembered how Dad had been with me the day of the fire, how we had winced at the disgusting smell of the creosote-soaked ties burning. Dad said something I didn't understand at first, but then I realized it must have come from his service in the Second World War. "You know," he said, walking faster as our nostrils filled with putrid smoke, "the smell of burning flesh, human flesh, you never forget it."

But Dad was not here now, and the thought of him was not going to deter me, was not going to dampen my enthusiasm for this momentous occasion. So I held onto the power of possibilities, the potential of the morning.

I held on past the boardwalk along Cooper's storefront to the gravelly edge of the road where the bus pulled in to pick up people going into town, from Langford through Colwood and over the Gorge into Victoria, BC.

On this day, an elderly lady looked askance at my sleeveless white blouse. "When I was a girl," she said, frowning, "we weren't allowed to show our bare arms." I thought she was being critical because she looked disapproving when she said, "Even in summer we had to wear long sleeves." But then she added "And it was so hot and so needless."

Stepping up into the bus, smiling at the driver and handing him the twenty-five cent fare there was only one thing that really mattered. Not what I wore or how I did my make up, or how I got to the audition. Just going—that was the thing.

❖　❖　❖

All kinds of girls show up for the audition, but when I see the girl in a Chanel suit I realize there's a whole other level of mother-daughter relationships. She has a fancy cosmetic case dangling from her wrist—you know the kind I mean; it's blue and it belongs to a luggage set, only it's small and rounded on the edges. I step into the elevator with her and her mom, who both have pink nail polish and blonde hair pinned up in French rolls. I'm a brunette, and because the mother-daughter look is bringing out my insecurities, I remind myself that Elizabeth Taylor, Sophia Loren and Audrey Hepburn are brunettes, also. Scrutinizing the daughter's heavy foundation, I'm thinking I should have put on more make up than just lipstick and mascara. They stand, perfectly erect, eyes front as if I'm invisible, looking so *Oak Bay*. I'm thinking I saw an ad for the pale green suit the girl is wearing in <u>Seventeen</u> magazine when the mom says, "Remember your elocution lessons, Alana. E-*nun*-ciate." After that, they zip it as if they don't want me to hear any hints that might help me out.

We ride up in silence, me in my itchy crinoline and my drindle skirt, black with big red poppies all around the bottom. It's one Mom brought home from the laundry; and suddenly it seems a little faded and I can feel how Mom's white blouse is big in the collar and a bit bunchy around the waist, where I tucked it in. Still, I tell myself, it's okay, I look good.

There are about fifteen of us in a room, all waiting nervously, some with their mothers or sisters. Miss Seventeen gets called first, but it isn't long before the mother and daughter team come back through the green door. One at a time, names are called. Girls check their lipstick, straighten their skirts and sashay in. And then they sashay right back out again.

It is just before lunch and there are only two of us left when a phone rings. I am afraid the phone call means auditions are over for the day, and I'm not sure I'll be able to get back tomorrow. The receptionist answers, speaks briefly, and then calls my name from the list she has in front of her.

I get up and walk to a dark wood door with an old brass knob. Pausing to wipe my hands on my skirt first, I grasp the knob and open the door to a room that is like nothing I have ever seen. It is a vast room lined with mirrors reflecting darkened windows above and aged hardwood floors below. Wow.

A guy about my age, he's real square. I can tell, because he's wearing a sweater vest and a khaki jacket and all the cool guys wear Jimmy Dean jackets, and ducktail hair like Elvis. Anyway, he's talking to an older guy—maybe thirty, maybe not that old, who's like, in charge.

The man setting this up introduces me to the kid, Timothy, who's going to be the leading man. We shake hands, and when Timothy smiles at me? It's nothing sexual, no physical attraction there, but my hands stop sweating, and I feel myself relax.

The older guy, Damion O, says they're still looking for the female lead. Damion has these dark intense eyes. "Alright, Margaret, it is Margaret, isn't it? Not Meg or Maggie?" I prefer Margaret and he says, "Alright then, let's see what you can do."

This is the moment I have waited for all my sixteen year-old life. The moment of truth. The moment that tells me if my dreams of being an actress are "just silly" like my mom says, or if they are grounded in reality, in real talent. So much of my life has been make-believe, pretending in order to survive the stultifying suffocation of being born into my family, of finding myself trapped in a baby-sitting, house-keeping, kept-in-the-yard world. I want out and this is my big chance.

This Damion guy tells us we're going to do an improvisation. It works like this; Damion gives us the low down about what's going on, a sort of scenario, and then we just make everything up, acting out the scene he has described. It's just play acting.

Right away, I relax. Like I said, make-believe is my specialty. Then I look over and see there's one of those big movie cameras and a guy running it. He's going to follow us around. It's a little unnerving but Tim's a natural, and I just follow his lead.

Margaret in wonderland,
looking-glass reflections,
movements perfecting lines
on polished sunlit floors
Timothy and I text flashing
between minds the rest of our lives
floating on lines concocted
while walking through dreams.
Floating reaching relaxed,
naturally talking, turning,
a touch, a laugh.
Diamond reflections
watch me I'm real
and you are the proof
for unbelievers.....see?
it's not just me.

Enchantment. That's it. Once on stage, it's like Tim and I are invisibly linked, mentally and physically. I can sense where he's going, and what sort of response he wants. It's as natural as smiling, as easy as being.

They run us through three more scenarios. Then Damion nods to the camera man, and then to another man who came in part way through, I guess, because I never noticed him before. Then Damion says, "Alright. Thanks, Margaret. We'll be in touch."

❖   ❖   ❖

I hurried down the gravel drive, eager to tell Grams about my film audition debut, but to my dismay, she stepped out onto the front porch in her best dress and hat.

"How did it go, dear?" she inquired politely.

"Fine, but there were a lot of girls trying out."

"I suppose there would be," she said and clucked her tongue as if to say, "too bad", while she checked her watch.

"You going out, Grams?"

"Mrs. Gray is picking me up. We're having tea at her place."

"That's nice. I think I did okay today. At the audition, I mean."

"Oh, good." A small gray Morris Minor pulled into the drive. Grams pulled on a pair of white cotton gloves, and turned to me, "Here's Mrs. Gray now, dear." As the Morris approached with the stout Mrs. Gray at the wheel, she added, "You won't forget the floor in Scotty's room needs washing?"

"I won't forget, Grams."

"You'll take care of it, then?"

"Sure, Grams," I said. I was disappointed. Not about having to wash the floor in Scotty's room—I'd known that before I set out. But I guess I thought she'd naturally want to know how things turned out.

It never occurred to me to refuse to wash the floor. In the Adam household it was not permitted to say no to Grams or to any adult. From birth I was trained to unconditional and unquestioning obedience of adult authority. This was further drilled into us in Baptist Sunday School sessions. Ephesians 6:1 was often quoted both at home and at church: "Children, obey your parents in the Lord, for this is right." No one ever went on to discuss verse four which talked about a father's responsibility to his children. The emphasis was all on the child's responsibility.

Besides, I knew all too well how it felt to be the target of an adult rage. Not that Grams ever went after me. All punishment ended up in the hands of my father. Even if he worked away, when he came home, I'd "get it" for a list of wrongs saved up by Mom or Grams or both.

This delayed punishment gave me the sensation of living in two worlds, one when dad was gone and everything seemed fairly stable, and another when he came home and we suddenly found we were 'in for it" for something we'd done some time ago. And if it was Grams who told on us, we wouldn't know until Dad addressed the situation. From the moment he pulled in the drive, we lived on tenterhooks, always wondering what our "due" was, if we would be lined up for the "strap" a thick leather belt he dealt upon our bare legs, or if it would just be a red-faced lecture. And always, we were careful what we said, cautious in case we'd inadvertently ignite his famous flashes of temper.

Parents ruled. As a daughter in the household, my role was to help the womenfolk, to obey my parents and elders, to be seen more than heard, and to generally "mind your P's and Q's".

To have told my grandmother I was not going to wash the floor would be the same as telling her I was going to the moon on Sputnik. She wouldn't have believed me for a second.

❖   ❖   ❖

July 23, 1963.
Dear Diary:

I auditioned for a National Film Board film today! We all sat in this big room waiting to be called, and when it was my turn I got to do three scenes, maybe fifteen, twenty minutes in all, and a lot of girls, actually all the girls before me came out a lot sooner, so like, maybe I have a chance.

When I got home, Grams asked me to scrub the floor in Scotty's room. I waltzed around, like Cinderella, sloshing the water, gliding the mop back and forth across the floor, pretending I was stage centre on Dick Clark's American Bandstand. Maybe I got the part, and maybe I didn't, but who cares? I've been to a real honest to goodness film audition!

Yours truly,
Margaret Jean.

CHAPTER 4

I knew about auditions. Not film auditions, but the usual high school drama club auditions. You showed up at the prescribed time, you read, and you watched for the director's response and hoped you'd done well enough to get a part.

For me, one of the most promising aspects of entering high school in grade seven was the existence of the drama club. While I cannot recall exactly at what point I had decided to become an actress, I can say definitively that it preceded my entry into the upper grades by quite a number of years, and I saw the drama club as the natural starting point for my career. So the call for auditions drew me like the need to spawn drives a salmon upstream.

As I entered the library, the room designated for try-outs, I noticed a short woman in a bright paisley artist's smock. What I remember as bright auburn curls thinly covered her scalp, and she cocked her head in conversation with a senior student, who I recognized as Anna Needham.

To their right, a man about the same height as the woman, dressed in a grey suit, coke-bottle eyeglasses, and a French beret gestured gracefully to a boy across the room. I recognized them as Mr. and Mrs. Ducaine, the school librarians, and obviously the drama teachers. You would have thought that I, wanting an acting career as desperately as I did, would have gone to any lengths to appease these guardians of the stage. But alas, my Asperger's kicked in.

It wasn't so bad at first, although when I heard that grade seven students were not permitted to read for speaking parts I must have made some outraged remark. There was a twitter of nervous giggles among the regulars in the club, and the Ducaines explained that familiarity with the physical stage and the ins and outs of being on stage with other players was vitally important and must precede the possibility of speaking parts.

My eagerness to get on with my acting career met this foil with little grace. However, I managed to behave sufficiently well for the rest of the afternoon to be awarded a small speechless part—one of the dancing dusky maidens.

My overall impression was that if you were a dusky maiden and managed your part well, the

Ducaines had promised you would then have an opportunity to read for the next play which would audition in the Spring. After all, you would then have familiarized yourself with the stage, and all of its ins and outs and be primed for an actual speaking role.

In all fairness to the Ducaines, this may simply have been my internal processing of the situation, and not anything actually verbalized. However, when the Spring try-outs came, and I was again refused the chance to read for a part, I made a strong and forthright statement expressing my keen disappointment and stormed out.

From then on, every Fall and every Spring in grades eight, nine and ten, I arrived at the library to audition. There was always a giggle when the Ducaines asked what part would I like to read? I always gave the same reply, "The female lead." They let me read. And every Fall and every Spring, when the results were posted, my name was conspicuously absent.

And then I started grade eleven to the terrific news that the Ducaines had retired.

The new drama teacher was a corker, a word my father used to describe astounding people and events. With shoulder-length blonde hair, tight skirts and sweater sets, Miss Charles perfectly suited the stiletto heels that announced her way down the hall and the little red convertible sports car which she drove to school.

She wafted into Belmont High on a wave of perfume and sunbeams. Young, brilliant and no-nonsense, Miss Charles' first priority was the grade eleven and twelve literature and language courses, an auxiliary to which was the Drama Club.

We were reading Shakespeare's Macbeth in class, aloud, and it was my turn to read. It was early on in the part where Lady Macbeth is nagging, provoking, humiliating her husband into killing his king. When I finished reading, it was quiet in the room. Miss Charles studied me in silence for a moment. Then she blinked and said, "We're having tryouts for the play on Thursday. I'd like you to come and read."

❖　❖　❖

But with regard to the film audition, I had no idea how long it would be before I knew whether or not I got the part. And judging by Miss Chanel, if money, class and wardrobe were factors, I could kiss my chances goodbye. But I could hope, couldn't I? As it turned out, the reality of that call was beyond even my wildest imagining.

CHAPTER 5

I was in up to my elbows in dishwater washing out the porridge pot, a job I always hated because of the slimy, starchy feel of the cooked oatmeal against my skin, when the call finally came. The ringing beckoned me to the other end of the house, to the front hall and the wall-mounted dial phone, as I hastily dried hands and arms on my apron, running just a little. I was slightly out of breath when I answered.

"Hello?"

"Miss Adam?"

"Yes."

"Margaret Adam?"

"Yes."

"This is Dick Sydowski from the National Film Board calling.

"Hello."

"Margaret, we'd like you to play the lead in our little film."

The earth did not move. The sky did not fall. But my soul did a swooping somersault in the sky and joy tingled through my fingertips.

"Oh, thank you! Oh that's great, that's wonderful, thank you so much!" Omigosh, how exciting!!! But I can't."

"Excuse me? You can't what?"

"Oh, I know it's a great honour, and believe me, I'm just so thrilled. But I couldn't possibly."

"I don't understand, Miss Adam."

"Well, you're probably filming downtown, right?"

"Right."

"And Mom and Dad took the car to Saskatchewan, you see my Uncle's dying, and I'm here at home looking after my grandmother, and she's fine if I go to work, but I have, well I just have no way to get there. To where you're filming, see?"

He didn't even hesitate. "Oh that's no problem. We'll have a car and driver pick you up every morning and bring you home every night."

Visions of Audrey Hepburn in *Breakfast at Tiffany's* swirled through my head. Omigosh! It was happening to me!

"You'll need certain wardrobe items of course, I have a list for you. A summer skirt and blouse and matching shoes, then a different outfit, a dress perhaps with a cardigan, or a light jacket, and another set of slacks—"

"Oh, Mr.—I'm sorry, what did you say your name was?"

"Sydowski."

"Mr. Sydowski, I have to bow out, I'm afraid. But thank you, thank you so much for choosing me. I'm so thrilled that you did."

"I don't understand?" I could hear a pencil tapping against a desktop.

"I'm really grateful. Just ever so, but I don't have a wardrobe. I borrowed my Mom's blouse to come to the audition, see, and the skirt? Well, one of the ladies from Mom's work gave it to her. If you need wardrobe, Mr. Sydowski, you have to pick somebody else. But thank you. It means a lot to me that I was your first choice."

There was a brief sigh on the other end of the phone. "Really, Miss Adam, may I call you Margaret?"

"Yes."

"In the film world, Margaret, these things are not important."

"You mean that what I have will do?"

"No. I mean we'll take you shopping."

Did I die right that very moment and go to heaven? Absolutely!

❖   ❖   ❖

As a girl, a teenage girl, I inhabited chasms of despair and rage, shifting radically to radiant heights of hope and certainty. My movements, exactly chronicled by my Grandmother, do not express that anger, bitterness and self-doubt, nor that sudden excess of exuberant confidence that would flood my sails and push me violently forward on life's journey.

And always, some thing, some little thing would happen, or maybe it was the absence of anything happening, and my ignorance of how to make it happen that unleashed my rampant insecurity, a devouring bestial emotion curled on the doorstep of my psyche, ready to spring in and overpower my desire to excel to succeed to fulfil that *Margaret Jeanness* that at some deep unspeakable level I believed was the quintessential me.

❖   ❖   ❖

By the summer I was sixteen, I had calmed down considerably. A lot of what had happened to me and the violent reaction I had when it was over seemed to seep away into some nebulous sphere.

In part, that was because Frank de Courcy had gone back to jail, and so I'd finally stopped going over to Eddy C's run down little cottage to skip classes.

My parents, my grandmother and myself, we all tried to pretend that nothing untoward had ever happened in our lives and we were just a normal happy family. But then reality would rear its ugly head and we'd be floundering again.

Thurs. July 25, 1963

We tidied and Marg Vacuumed. Worked at garden. A man came re: Marg's T.V. job. Nice card from Mrs. Kieler, and letter re funeral from Alice.

Friday, July 26, 1963

Marg downtown all day re: the T.V. show. She and Mgr. Tried to shop for dresses etc. but nothing suitable so to Vancouver tomorrow. Nicky to go along to drive through city.

Mr. Sydowski asked if someone was available to act as chaperone on the trip to Vancouver.

Someone else might have suggested a maiden aunt. At least hesitated. Exhibited some caution. But Asperger's me, I just piped right up: "I have a boyfriend, Nick. He's seventeen."

"He'll do nicely."

Sat. July 27, 1963

Up before 5 AM Marg early breakfast & ready, Nicky came & they met up with Mr. Kowalski & on to Vancouver. Shopped for Marg's part in show. No mail. To Coopers' for a few supplies.

In the shops, it quickly became apparent that I had little experience shopping for clothes. Sydowski, a pleasant, paternal man, soon realized I had no idea about suitable undergarments, or mix and match outfits. He was a genius at setting me up with the sales clerks, and if we got one that was a bit uppity with me, we soon exited the store, without purchases.

I don't remember much that we bought; a yellow silk chambray pleated skirt, a brown and yellow silk floral blouse, a red/teal and yellow paisley cotton blouse, teal stretch slacks—those I remember. I know we bought shoes, slips, hosiery, and undergarments for each outfit. My hair was left as it was, and I said I was okay for make up.

In the whirlwind of shops and dining, everything was a blur. Nick, who had traveled extensively with his family, church and the school band, was quite at ease. He was probably the most socially adept person in my limited circle of friends, and therefore, a good choice of companion. My grandmother certainly thought highly of him. *Nicky*[9].

July 27, 1963. Saturday,
Dear Diary;

All I can say is: Oh God Please don't let me wake up from this. Please don't take this away from me. Oh God Please don't let Mom and Dad come home and end this incredible romantic adventure. Thank you thank you Lord!

Yours truly,
Margaret Jean.

UNFORGIVING

Ferries plying the water to dress shops
lingerie
silks
knits
unraveling
trade routes
of the heart
beating
paths to
dreamy identity
doors swinging open
fierce heart
hoping
it won't
end
too soon

CHAPTER 6

Sun. July 28, 1963.

Nicky & family took Marg to church A.M. The two out for awhile afternoon. M. pressed dresses etc. ready for tomorrow. Watered a lot. Roses budding again.

❖　❖　❖

Church was a constant in my life. I was six years old when Mr. Clifford Padgett in the brow-wiping heat of a summer's day showed up at our back door, asking if there were any children home who might like to go to Sunday School. A little olive-skinned man, Mr. Padgett and his determination mightily impressed my mother, and so it was decided that Rob, my nine year old brother, and I were to attend the little brown Baptist Church every Sunday even though the family was Anglican. It wasn't like we were abdicating—at least not physically. Although my grandmother attended Anglican services every Sunday without fail, and although we had been christened in the Anglican church, for some reason, neither my parents nor us children accompanied Grams to the 'Church of England' as she described it. And if Mr. Padgett won the right to teach us in Sunday school, he failed to attract my parents, who perhaps came once or twice on unremembered occasions.

So from 1955 until the September I married D.B. in its shadowy interior in 1964, I walked the mile and a half to church every Sunday, sang the hymns with zest, and listened intently to the Bible story and messages about baby Moses hidden in the bulrushes, about Noah building the giant Ark and best of all about how Jesus came to earth, God made human, to take our sins on his brutalized body and give us all eternal life. What a wonderful story! And the best part was that it was *true*.

You see, I had asked about that in Sunday school, did the historians know about Jesus? And Mrs. Padgett in her red stiletto heels and perfectly tailored suit had said yes, it was recorded history that Jesus died for us and rose again. And Mom and Dad agreed, and so did Grams. So it had to be true. And God loved me, Jesus loved me, and there were angels all around me. So no matter

what happened at school, however alone or belea-
guered I felt, how out of my depth and all on my
own, it was inconsequential because God was
omnipotent and he was with me everywhere and
he thought I was worth dying for.

Wow. What a break for a socially challenged
kid. As the years went by, the gospel message
seeped deep into my psyche, until finally, with all
the enthusiasm and inspiration of a ten year old
with Asperger's, I began parroting Mr. Padgett's
sermons, "reaching out" to the kids at school. But
this alone was not enough to satisfy my new-found
religious fervor. I hastily penned long preachy letters to all my cousins in Saskatchewan, hoping to
save them from the fires of hell and damnation.
After all, they were family, and it was up to me to
save their souls. Naturally, I did not mention any of
this to my parents. I just assumed they would be
alright with it.

Then the letters began arriving. A regular flurry
of white envelopes with Saskatchewan postmarks,
from my Aunts and Uncles. Probably more amused
than outraged, nevertheless, they demanded that
my father put an end to my appeals. I vividly recall
the conversation.

I had cut through from Jenkins (then Jacklin)
Road along a wide dirt path to the tracks, singing

gospel songs at the top of my lungs; *What A Friend We Have In Jesus* was one of my favorites for obvious reasons. I belted out the songs in the hope that anyone within earshot would be converted by the words, or at least stop me to ask questions about the wonderful message contained therein. Naturally, no-one did.

I crossed the tracks and took the narrow path down to Station Road and wound up the journey home with a rousing rendition of *Onward Christian Soldiers*. When I burst in through the back door and swung up the hallway into the kitchen, Dad and Mom were waiting for me, their faces set. Instantly, I knew I was in for it. I just had absolutely no idea why.

"Sit down, Margy," Dad said. I sat, my stomach feeling all tight and queer. "Have you been writing to your cousins about religion?" Puzzled, I nodded. "Yes." I said.

"Well stop it for heaven's sakes!"

I wanted to reply it was for heaven's sake I was doing it. But I knew better than to reply. Any reply other than "Yes sir" would have meant instant punishment, severe in the heat of his anger. Undoubtedly, I looked stunned. Shocked. I probably stood there with my mouth open and my head spinning.

"Can't you see you're embarrassing the whole family?" he asked, his disbelief equal to mine.

"But, Dad," I began.

"For Pete's sake, just stop it!" Dad demanded.

While any other child might have taken Mr. Padgett's passionate exhortations about "go forth and preach the gospel" as mere pulpit rhetoric, the notion that the little man was not sincere did not occur to me. Nor to Mr. Padgett, who when I wrote him forty years later, told me he and his wife prayed for me every Saturday all of their lives.

And even at the tender age of ten, I could not for the life of me reconcile this moment to the beliefs and values I thought my family held. After all, Mom had sent me to church because Mr. Padgett had come to our house and spoken to us about Jesus and his love, so presumably it was a good thing to talk to strangers about God. Taking it one step further, how much better then, to reach out to the people you cared about, to bring them the "good news". My father, drunk and sober, often launched into lectures not just on larger moral issues such as right and wrong, but emphatic, Bible-pounding sermons on God, his son, Jesus and the devil.

In true Asperger's isolation, I was stymied. I had taken the little enthusiastic preacher literally, and gone out to tell "all the world" about God's love for us. And once again, become an embarrassment and disappointment to my family. And how? By doing exactly what they had given every indication was not only the right, but the necessary thing to do.

All the music flowed out of me, all the words of comfort and praise drained away as if I were a bathtub and someone had just pulled the plug. Within the circle of God's love, I had felt as if I finally belonged to a community, felt bonded with my family, as if in this one sense we were finally a united front.

But Dad's instruction, and the obvious displeasure I felt from both parents cut me loose, and I was again a single small craft, adrift, without anchor or moorage, unable to navigate within even the small social circle of my family. For a brief moment, I felt humiliated and alone, as if God had never loved me, as if I was not worthy of his great sacrifice, as if it were all something too silly to be believed.

But as I went to my room, I thought about God and his son and their love for me, and the feeling that flowed through me was so real, I could neither ignore nor deny it. If my parents didn't want me to talk about God or share with others this overwhelming sense of love and blessing, then, I wouldn't. But my long and constant conversations with God would not cease. My songs of praise would not be dampened.

Still, I lay on my bed feeling as if I had rocks in my gut.

❖   ❖   ❖

Gardening was another constant in our lives. I think back to those summer days and I can see my grandmother in her straw hat, thick, beige cotton stockings and black lace up, high-heeled gardening shoes and flowered housedress. "Housedress"— that special, homely garment, usually shirt-waisted and front buttoning with a flared skirt, originally bright in color and pattern, now faded from the rigors of the wringer washing machine.

For some reason, the gardening, along with mending and quilt-making fell to Grams. She labored daily, sowing, weeding, hoeing, staking and tying up. As well as half an acre of vegetables, she grew marvelous blooms. The perfume of her roses was exquisite, and our house was redolent with the fragrance of her bouquets all summer long. Her favorite was the pale yellow Peace rose with its pink blush; but she also coaxed the stunning red "American Beauty" rose into massive heads, along with various pinks.

UNFORGIVING

Once, not long ago, one summer afternoon, walking with my Mother (years after Grams' passing), I came upon a private garden in Vancouver's West End. Benches set in amongst lush rose bushes beckoned us, roses with luxuriant orange heads. When I saw those orange roses, bred and marketed years after Grama's death, I wished she could be walking with us.

Perhaps she was. Perhaps she did see, from some unique perspective, the brilliant, heavy heads, bowed and flared, petals spilling everywhere, my mother bending to smell the delicious scent, reaching to touch the silky petals.

CHAPTER 7

Mon. July 29, 1963.

Marg to studio at 8:30 home 6 p.m. Had shopped for 4 prs. Nylons. Nicky brought her home. I washed all laundry, fed[b] cheque to bank, paid up all utilities. Marian, Una & Edna wrote, card from Dot and Gil. Nicky sanded doors.[c]

The wondrous day started when Mr. Sydowski arrived in a sleek black rental car. He had phoned the night before to give me "wardrobe", and I wore the skirt and sweater outfit.

"Sunny today, 'ey?" Sydowski remarked as I slid in the front seat beside him. "It could get a little hot under the lights," he added. As if I cared.

---

b Fed: an abbreviation for "federal" meaning, I assume, the old age or Canada pension cheque.

c Nicky sanded doors?

On the way to the location, what Sydowski termed "the shoot", we stopped to pick up a gangly kid named Bernie, about nineteen.

Once on set, Damion gave us the run down of how we were to proceed. First we were given a script to study. The parts weren't very long. And while we were doing that, the cameramen and the director figured out the sequence of the movements that would accompany the lines. Nothing would be marked, except where we started from—which was marked with white "X's" chalked on the floor.

The first time we got in front of the cameras, and on ours marks, I was really nervous. Then a guy came out with this slate thing that he clapped down, and the director yelled "Action" and Tim started with his lines. As soon as Tim started talking, I found myself easily transported in the make believe of it all. But sometimes the lines were worded quite differently, or the movements seemed to oppose the lines, and then we had to redo the scene.

Once it took us four takes and we still didn't get it right. Tim and I were pretty appalled.

Smith heard us worrying about how we must do it right next time, and laughed.

"You guys are worried about four takes?"

We nodded miserably.

"That's nothing. Don't worry over that. You ever watch the Ozzie and Harriet Show?"

"Sure!" Everybody did.

Smith grinned. "Well one time we were doing an ad with Ozzie and it took him thirteen takes to do the scene."

Thirteen takes? That made us feel better. But since both Tim and I had competitive natures, we were still determined to get it right next time. And we did.

I wanted to know about the movie we were doing.

"It's not exactly a movie," Damion told me. "It's what they call a 'short'; when it's all done it'll only be about twenty minutes long."

"So where will it be shown then?" I asked.

"In schools. It's for high school kids. The working title is 'Stay in School'."

Damion went on to explain that it's sort of a drama for kids who want to drop out, like my big brother, Rob, did in grade ten.

This is meant to convince them otherwise, because dropping out is supposedly bad for your future. Tim plays my boyfriend, and he wants to drop out of school, and I'm supposed to be ready to break up with him over it.

As if I would ever leave a guy for such a dumb reason. I mean, if you love somebody, you love them no matter what right? What does money have to do with it? Geez, according to them, then, Mom shoulda left Dad eons ago!

Anyway, Damion, the too charming assistant director, takes us aside to run through the scene. We do a couple of rehearsals and then we do the take. The lighting and set up takes forever and we don't have fancy trailers to relax in or anything like in the movie magazines.

We just work our lines on the side, and stand around and gab in between. Today we filmed in some building called the studio. I have no clue where[10].

My head was totally in the clouds, except for when I was focused on the script. Like totally.

About 4:30 I phoned Nick from the set.

"Hello, Nick, how are you?"

"I'm good. How's the starlet?"

"Terrific. Doing okay. We're going to be finished about five o'clock today."

"I can pick you up if you want?"

"Just a minute, I'll ask if it's okay."

Sydowski said fine, and gave Nick directions. A little while later Nick showed up, his silver blue 1932 Austin Healey, turning heads.

I was exhausted from being "on" all day. More than anything, I wanted to eat and go to bed. And unbelievably, Grams had dinner ready. I mean, she always made dinner with me for Mom and Dad, but now there was just the two of us, and I was a kid, I was like the underling, and here she made dinner for me. "A light supper" she called it. Salad and a bit of chicken and some fruit. Perfection. She fed Nick, too, who hung around to sand a door that Grams said was sticking.

Nick chucked my chin and grinned at me. "Some big star, all tuckered out!"

As soon as Nick left, Grams asked for my stockings and bra etcetera. This was an odd request.

"My underwear?"

"Yes, you'll want it to be fresh tomorrow. If you give it to me, I'll rinse it out. It should be dry by morning."

I was truly moved by that homely offer. Grams, who rang her bedside bell whenever she wanted more tea or had an errand that needed running. Imagine, Grams doing something so menial for me!

And then she asked what I wanted for breakfast tomorrow.

"Cornflakes if we have any, please," I requested, thinking silently to myself, *Just not the usual lumpy porridge, please!*

❖   ❖   ❖

Even today, for me, exhaustion is the hallmark of any event requiring social interaction. This is largely due to my Asperger's which was exacerbated by the rules at home.

Although we were schooled in manners, as children we were not generally engaged in conversation. Children were "seen and not heard" in our family as in doubtless many others of the day. This precluded practice at social communication. Since the radio news broadcast aired at five p.m., pretty much the exact time we sat down to dinner, we often ate in silence for the duration of the program so our parents could keep abreast of local and world events.

Having Asperger's did not help the situation. More often than not, when I did speak it was to voice some inappropriate sentiment or make some off the mark comment.

Although I was well read and easily comprehended books like Shakespeare and the King James Bible, I was unable to pick up on conversationally inferred meanings, and generally took any conversation as being word for word reliable. This made me appear gullible and not particularly bright at times.

Take for instance, the time our coach, Harold Banks, showed up in our locker room.

There were all kinds of teachers at our school. Two opposite extremes were Mr. Peach and Mr. Banks.

Mr. Peach, to my way of thinking, was practically a saint. See, when we went up to high school, black and white saddle shoes were the trend. Every kid wore them. I personally hated them, because I had very narrow feet and the oxfords or saddle shoes only came in wide to medium.

I don't recall at what point they became popular, but I know I suffered them from elementary into high school. Not the same pair of course, my mother was very good about getting me a new pair of shoes every fall for school. But I had narrow feet—triple A's—shoes with far less demand and therefore, far higher price. And apparently there was no such thing as "narrow" fitting oxfords.

So I slopped along in the cheaper, sturdier saddle shoes, my feet blistering and bleeding for the first two weeks or so until they toughened up. It might have helped if I would have worn socks with them but the trend at the time was to wear none, and that only exasperated the situation. If it hadn't been for Mr. Peach, I honestly don't know what kind of problems I might have had with my feet.

I cannot recall his first name; we wouldn't dream of referring to a teacher that way. I do remember his red hair, his roman nose, his kind eyes. He seemed to me a tall man, very much a man's man. In my memory he wears tweed jackets and sweater vests and grey slacks, and smokes a pipe. He must have been my grade seven home room teacher, though I am not certain of that either. Whatever our scholastic relationship, he saved my feet.

Early in grade seven (we went up to high school in grade seven then, there was no middle school and no junior high), I came limping into school with blood running down the back of my shoes and my feet. It honestly never occurred to me that showing up at school with bloody feet and shoes was an issue. I had no concept of how I looked to others, or how my unkempt appearance might affect others' opinions of me. Nonetheless I protested.

"I *hate* oxford shoes," I declared at the shoe store.

Mom crossed her arms and said, "Well, that's what you're going to get."

At home, I appealed to Dad. "These shoes are so ugly, Dad." His face got red. On the one hand, appearances were important to Dad. On the other hand, he knew that my taste was sometimes quite off the mark. He'd seen the other kids, lots of them, wearing oxfords as they walked past our house to school.

"I think they look pretty nice," he said.

I groaned and threw myself back in the big brown chair.

"Now, none of that, now!" he said sternly. "You're to wear those shoes and that's it!"

I don't know how my parents didn't see the problem. We were chastened to wear our shoes in the house—to take them off was forbidden—Dad said only "foreigners" took their shoes off in the house. Good Canadian stock kept their shoes on. So maybe I changed into my old shoes when I got home. That would have been encouraged by my elders, because saving money and keeping your "good clothes" for school and church, clean and wearable, was very important.

And my feet didn't start bleeding at the front door. It wasn't until I was down the road and the blisters had time to form and burst that the problem began. So my parents and Grams most likely never saw any problem with the shoes, other than my personal taste.

But Mr. Peach noticed. I don't know if he waited until recess or if he just wheeled me down to the first aid room the moment I got into class. But once there he filled a basin with warm water, took some soap and a cloth and bade me sit on a chair and take off my shoes. To my surprise, he took my foot in his hand and began washing it.

"Doesn't it hurt?" he asked.

"Only the first bit. By the time I get to school, it's okay."

"Why don't your parents buy you proper fitting shoes?" he asked irritably, drying my feet and removing and rinsing out the basin.

"They can't afford it. Dad's out of work now for the winter, so we have to be careful," I told him.

"Give me your foot," he said, and I put it back in his hands, and he carefully bandaged over the blister. "Now the other one," he said when he finished.

I went to slip my feet back into my shoes. "Uh-uh-uh!" he admonished, and took the shoes to the sink and carefully cleaned them with the damp cloth.

"Here you go, Margaret," he said, and helped me put them on. "Do you have Bandaids at home?" he asked.

Of course we did. We had little kids, didn't we, always falling down and scraping knees or elbows.

"Well, you put a couple of bandaids on those blisters before you leave for school."

I did, too, but they often wore off before I got halfway down the hill by Hull's farm. And then I'd end up back in the first aid room with Mr. Peach. He was the kindest man I ever met. And professional. Nothing untoward at all in what he did for me.

Not like Harold Banks.

CHAPTER 8

Harold Banks was blue-eyed and had an unruly thatch of blond hair, which combined with freckles and chubby cheeks gave him an artless, boyish look. He taught Art and Gym and had the reputation of being a masher. In art class, if he was demonstrating how to hold a pencil, he'd sit in the small desks beside the girls and put his arm around them and proceed to hold their hand in his while making the drawing motion.

"He's a creep," Matt Mahoney, our foremost art student, told me as we were leaving class one day. I think Matt realized I was not too bright about social situations. "Don't let him do that to you. He doesn't need to put his arm around you to show you anything." Some of the girls outright resisted him.

Like Jenina, my friend from Millstream Road. Jenina and I had both lived way down the end of

Millstream Road when we were little, before my family moved to the house on Station Road, after my grandfather died, in 1952. But in Millstream, my family lived in two houses, a larger house which Mom and Dad and my older brother and I lived in, and a smaller cottage style house which Grams and Grampa had down by the creek. Now, at Station Road, Grams lived with us in our house, but from the time I was old enough to remember until I was six, Jenina and I played in the woods behind and the fields beside our Millstream homes.

We were friends when we started school, and there Jenina realized she was a lot more popular than I was. Then the friendship dynamic shifted. I had been bossy and assumed leadership of our playtime at home, but at school, she prevailed, and often went off with other children to play games to which I was not invited. It was no big deal. I liked to be by myself anyway, and Jenina would occasionally play with me as well. And we continued to be friends at home, right through Belmont High School.

If we stayed late after school we would sometimes go into old Alex Shovovo's general store (right across from Belmont) and buy pomegranates. Then we'd sit side by side on the school fence, peeling the leathery red rinds, and picking out the jewel-like seeds, the red juice staining our hands and chins.

We had two things in common, Jenina and I. We both had alcoholic dads and we both loved sports. We often wound up walking home together simply because we were on the same team, and after-school practices meant we were leaving much later than the other kids she hung out with. We played basketball and softball—she was much better at softball than I, and I was often a second stringer. I think after grade eight, I probably didn't even make the team. But we were both on the basketball team pretty much all through high school.

Mr. Banks was inclined to keep the two of us after practice to shoot some extra free throws or practice certain shots. I don't remember how it began, but I do remember Jenina and I walking casually from the gym to the girl's locker room door, and then, the instant we were through, breathlessly turning the lock. "That'll keep Banks out," Jenina said. So for sure Banks had once taken the liberty of wandering into the locker room through the gym door when we were in the showers.

From then on, whenever he kept the two of us late after practice we made sure to lock him out. Things were okay for awhile, but sometime later, we were safely in the showers. The gym door was securely locked.

"What was that?" I asked, turning off the water.

"Huh?" Jenina looked at me. Then realization struck. "It's the G----m door to the hall!"

For one brief moment we stared at each other in amazement. The same thought struck us both at once: though the door to the gym could be locked, the door to the main hallway of the school could not—except by key. And students were not issued keys. Ergo, Harold Banks could enter through that door anytime he pleased.

"Don't worry girls, I'm just here to pick up the equipment."   His statement came off as a casual remark, as if it was the most natural thing in the world for a male coach to be in the girls' locker room, and we shouldn't be alarmed.

❖   ❖   ❖

I have read that the average person places trust based 55% on body language, 38% on tone, and a mere 7 % on words. People with Asperger's have trouble with the non-verbal aspects of language. Differentiating pitch, tone and other interpretive clues to language is something we need to be taught, which means that initially? Trust is based almost entirely on the spoken word, as if the words were a direct and infallible message. In other words, our method of verbal communication is not sophisticated and is the exact opposite approach of most non-Asperger people.

The inability to grasp what to others are obvious nuances of a conversation puts a person, at best, in a difficult position and at worst, at risk.

❖   ❖   ❖

I was suddenly confused; he was a teacher—a male figure of authority, and I was well versed in authority figures. Both my parents and the Bible and Emily Post's big book of Etiquette said authority figures were to be obeyed. Without question. And he *said* it was okay for him to be there.

It was the Asperger's kicking in again, taking the verbal as gospel. It is the only part of communication we really connect with. What he said was more significant to me than how he was behaving. I was uncertain what to think.

Not Jenina. She lit into a violent rage—"Banks, you f-----g asshole, you f------g pervert, you get the hell out of here or I'll report you, you miserable piece of shit, you f----g pig, you! Get out! Get out right now, or I'll report you to Svenson. F---k off! Move! Get out!"

Asperger me, I protested. "Jenina," I said as Banks slipped back out into the hallway, "that's no way to talk to a teacher!"

"Are you an idiot or something?" she asked irritably. "He's a g_____d pervert. What do you think he's doing in here?"

I shrugged. I honestly didn't know. He was a *teacher.*

"Well *think* about it." She suggested, truly annoyed by my thick-headedness.

I felt tremendous dismay. I had been able to trust Mr. Peach. It never for one moment occurred to me not to.

If only someone could invent a behaviour decoder for me, I thought. Special glasses like superman wears, only instead of X-ray vision that lets you see through physical bodies, they would give me the lowdown on people's intentions. Show me not just the actions and words of the people around me, but visualize what these words and facial expressions and body language *meant.* Zing it instantly into my brain, you know? And then I wouldn't look so stupid all the time. I'd know how to respond appropriately, instead of standing here stuck in the indecision of being dependant on verbal cues alone.

Yes, Richie had repeatedly molested me, but the truth is, in my mind, I put people in separate compartments. Richie was a neighbour, a family friend. Watch out for all of the above. But a teacher? Those well-educated people who practised a profession in which they were given the care and trust of children? Teachers could prey on children?

I couldn't grasp the enormity of it. I wanted Jenina to be wrong, because if she was right, the paranoia and anger which stalked me at home would pervade my school time, which in spite of its social challenges had become a sexually neutral place for me. At least I didn't have to worry about someone like Richie waiting around every corner. And yet, after that, we locked the door to the gym and one of us stood guard by the hallway door, while the other showered. I think we treated it like a joke. "Watch out for that pervert, Banks."

Amazing, the human capacity for denial.

CHAPTER 9

Wed. July 31, 1963.

Mr. Sawatsky came at 7:18 AM for Marg. They did the "Royal Roads scene AM to PM He brought her home. I defrosted fridge & dusted, and also made soap. Marg & Nicky out eve. Prov. Cheque and Ingrid sent card.

July 31, 1963. Wednesday.
Dear diary.

Today was the pits. Guess where we were filming? Royal Roads. In the Castle. You know——that officer's training school. I got in trouble today.

It's emotionally draining this film business. I'm never quite sure where I'm at, but it always feels like I'm in the bottom of a tea-cup world looking up and seeing bits of "out" beyond the rim, and not really getting the full picture. As if I truly belong in a very small corner of the world, and I run smack into trouble every time I try to pull myself up.

I was worried sick they would fire me, so it was a relief Mr. E said, "So, see you tomorrow, Margaret? Same time?"

The minute I got in, I called Nick, and we drove to Metchosin, to the lagoon, natch, in the big old Hudson and parked. He lectured me. Told me I should have known better, and how I have to act professional. I was miffed, but then he took me in his arms and kissed me. And the boy can kiss.

Yours truly, (sigh)
Margaret Jean.

❖   ❖   ❖

It was the kind of day where your stockings stick to your legs and you hope your deodorant does what all the ads say it will do. Standing in front of big aluminum reflector panels, I could feel little rivulets of sweat crawling down my skin. I was wearing a yellow sun dress, a shirt waist with a full embroidered skirt, and high-heeled shoes. The sleeves were very short, and the assistant director, Damion, threw his jacket over my shoulders when he noticed a light burn starting on my arms. For most of the day, we filmed outside on deck on a destroyer.

Later, we moved to the castle grounds. It was blistering hot, and I was exhausted, so while we waited for the crew to set up, I ducked into the castle.

I didn't know it then, but the military academy was actually housed in Hatley Castle, a Castle built by Robert Dunsmuir, a coal baron, in the late 1800's. To me, it was like finding myself in a Disney movie—Cinderella at the ball, or Sleeping Beauty before she was banished. I recall being inside the castle…

The rooms were cool and spacious, and dark, ornate furniture sat in the rooms as if they had not been disturbed for a hundred years. On the walls, huge gilt-framed portraits stared unsmilingly at some distant point, and beneath them, exquisitely patterned carpets sprawled on perfectly polished parquet floors.

Like Alice in Wonderland, I wandered from room to room, peeking into each with awe, until finally I came upon a room where the sun slanted in the windows in the friendliest way, just as it did at home on the big brown chair where I curled up to read. So I slipped off my shoes and tucked my feet up under me and lay my head on the arm of a massive, and very comfy sofa.

At first I was alone and it was very pleasant, but shortly thereafter, a grey haired old geezer in a blue uniform, what they call a commission-aire, came through and gave me a look. I thought maybe the pins had come loose in my French roll or something, so I tucked them up. He left.

Not long after, in comes a man in a uniform, with a white hat and lots of trim on his jacket. With him is Mr. Smith, the director. They march in, Smith, too, like he's just been recruited, and they march right up to me and then stop. I felt like Queen Elizabeth or someone terribly important. I was waiting for them to salute when Smith said, "Miss Adam, you will please put your shoes on and put your feet flat on the floor. Where do you think you are?"

I could feel myself shrinking smaller and smaller inside like Alice in Wonderland. My face got all hot and I knew I was going beet red. I was about to die, so I made like I could care less. I sat as straight and tall as I could sit, my feet still curled under me and said, "But my feet aren't dirty."

Smith went beet red. He looked exactly like Dad when he says, "Don't you back-talk me!" So I knew the scenario. I looked him straight in the eye, slid my feet to the floor and said, "I'm sorry, Mr Smith. It won't happen again."

"It'd better not!" Smith turned on his heel and left, his neck redder than my face—my one consolation. Anyway, I half expected the officer to wink or something, but he did not seem to find the situation at all amusing.

Traveling between two worlds
little woman girl
embarrassed
and feigning aloof
who waits for her
who bends to hear
her sighs her dreams
who stoops to lift
her out of despair
where is her heart?
Skating on ice
as sheer as the wind
flying in the face
of a life
wanting in
and now she's through
blue eyes skies moods
waiting waiting waiting
to belong unable to find
that place
troubled triumphant mind
searching changing reaching
all the time.

CHAPTER 10

Fri. Aug. 2, 1963

Birnie drove Marg at 7:30 AM to work. I canned 4 qts Apricots but overcooked. To Coopers for groc. Nicky took Marg to Princess Mary[d] for dinner.

August 2, 1963. Friday.
Dear diary:

On Wednesday, Bernie got his car out of the garage. It's a cute little red sportscar. Wow. Anyway, he said he would drive me, since he lives in Belmont Park. You know, he has to come back a couple of miles to Langford to get me. Which is nice of him. Really. Except he drives like a maniac. But then, what are sports cars for?

---

d The Princess Mary was built in 1910 in Scotland, served as a coastal steamer along the BC coast until her retirement in 1951. Part of her superstructure serves as the Princess Mary Restaurant, 958 Harbour Rd. in Victoria, BC. In 1963, it was *the* place to dine.

So tonight Nick took me out to the Princess Mary. Since we finished the shoot at noon, and I was home by one, I had time to get ready; bubble bath, make up, the works. Nick gave a little whistle when I walked into the living room. Dad looked up from his paper and grinned. Nick gave me a little swat on the butt and said, "C'mon girl, we're late." I love it when he's like that. Makes me feel like we belong together.

Mostly we talked about the ecumenical conference coming up, and what's going on with his family. I like Nick. Sometimes I think we will probably get married, since my family likes him a lot, but then I remember his Mom, Mrs. W., and that time last Spring she got me a job in the cafe where she works—the Green Spot. You know, the one in Colwood Corners. Clark[11] says it should be called the "Grease Spot" (giggle). There was all that trouble and I quit. Remember that, dear diary? Sometimes I wonder if I could be happy married to Nick because of his mom. How would we ever get along?

But that's just silly. Because I love him soooooooo much.

Yours truly,
Margaret Jean.

❖   ❖   ❖

My shift started after school, so as soon as basketball practice was over, I hurried home, ate a plate of stew and Mom's baked bread, changed and headed out. The café was a small building sitting at the junction of the two main roads that give Colwood Corners its name, and backing on the golf course. Not nearly close enough to have any kind of view. It wasn't that kind of joint. Nick's mom, Mrs. W. was a thin, efficient woman, who bided no nonsense. From what Nick had told her she somehow got the impression that I was a spoiled baby and she was either intent on toughening me up or getting me out of her son's life. At least, that was the impression I got.

It was early on in my shift, and I was waiting on this old man. His breath whistled through his nose, he was stinking drunk, and he kept grabbing me, patting my buttocks and trying to put his arm around me.

For most women, being man-handled by a drunken stranger might be just a laughable incident, but for someone who has been the victim of sexual abuse, it is far from laughable. Every alarm bell goes off inside you, your skin literally crawls. Your chest goes tight. You feel like you can't get any air.

When I went in the back to put his order in, I told Mrs. W. I didn't want to serve him. She looked me straight in the eye and said, "One thing you had better learn—the customer is always right." My jaw dropped so far, it hit my knees.

But I clammed up and went to get a coffee for the old coot. I was so mad I was shaking, and I slammed the coffee pot back on the burner, and it started to fall. I reached up to catch it and hot coffee spilled all over my hand. I shrieked, and Mrs. W. told me to be quiet, it was nothing. With a disapproving glare, she soaked a towel in cold water and wrapped it around my hand. She took the coffee and delivered it to the customer.

When she came back into the kitchen she handed me an order pad. "Get back out there," she told me. "They're ready to order."

"I quit."

"Just because of a little burn?" She was truly disgusted with me.

"No." I said. "Just because of that lousy drunk out there. Nobody touches me. Nobody. You couldn't pay me enough to let somebody touch me like that!"

Mrs. W. stood in the doorway, hands on her hips, a flash of anger in her eyes. She had no way of knowing that when I was a little kid, eleven years old, I'd been in a position where I felt I had no choice about men touching me. She couldn't know that I had promised myself then that no dirty old man would ever touch me again.

❖   ❖   ❖

CHAPTER 11

In the summer of 1958, I was eleven years old, skinny like a pencil, barely five feet tall. Summers and after school, I helped my grandmother look after Terry and Scotty, keep the house and gardens while Mom and Dad went out to work. Because of Gram's frail health and my young age, I was confined to home. Once in awhile, I would get to babysit my cousins, who lived in Happy Valley in a rambling two-story house with a shingle exterior painted a rather muddy shade of pink. Dad had not quit drinking yet; that didn't happen until too late, until I was 13 and already ruined.

At this time, when I was eleven, we rented out the cabin, a little turquoise and brown two bed-room structure that Dad and my uncles built across the yard from our house. Maria and her husband rented it later, before they got divorced. Everyone who ever lived in our cabin got divorced. Even

Richie, who was our first tenant. Richie was a wiry, red-headed, army guy, with a huge smile and freckles that made him seem boyish and innocent.

I remember his wife, Andrea. I'd go over when Richie wasn't home, watch her brush "Cherry pink" polish on her long, perfectly shaped nails, and she'd ask my opinion as she tried different earrings and bracelets. The little cabin was always spotless, and it seemed to me that Andrea and their brown-eyed little girls spent their days in restless anticipation of Richie's return.

He liked to tease, even teasing my grandmother when the adults played canasta, everyone sitting around the kitchen table laughing and smoking, Grams asking people to "be serious" and "pay attention, now". Coffee and beer and Richie's favorite, Vodka, were imbibed, while Richie and Dad traded hints across the table about what cards to hold and what to lay down, much to Gram's fury and Maria's amusement. Sometimes they were short a hand and then I got to play.

At first, it wasn't any fun because I was too young and not aware of the refinements of the game, and the adults got upset if I made a play that gave the opposing team a clear advantage. But by the time I was eleven, I had caught on and finally had the delicious pleasure of "going out" on Richie and Dad, of laying down my cards and ending the hand.

Which got Richie's attention. That was when he first noticed me. Began to think of me in other ways.

One night when the kitchen table was littered with bottles of vodka, rum, beer and Crown Royal, when Mom sat on a stool pumping "Red Sails in the Sunset" out of her accordion, Dad waltzing Kitty Desmarais around the living room, I came out of the bathroom at the end of the hall and walked right smack into Richie.

I was startled and before I could apologize, he grabbed me by the shoulders and kissed me hard. To my astonishment, I felt his tongue in my mouth.

I tried to scream and push him away, but he held me firm, his tongue thick and dirty inside me. At first I flailed and pounded, too frightened to think. Then instinctively I sensed that he enjoyed the struggle, so I relaxed, and to my relief, after a moment or two, he withdrew, let go, laughed at me when I wiped my mouth with the back of my hand and said, "You're getting to be a big girl now," and went into the bathroom.

Outraged, I went into the kitchen and told my aunt, "Richie French-kissed me."

A group of women were standing there. My Mom's sister, Aunt Rose, who worked at the telephone office, my Dad's sister, Aunt Nell, and some others, I don't recall exactly who. They all burst out laughing as one. "Don't be silly, Marg." Before continuing their conversation someone asked, "Isn't it time you were in bed?"

"But he did!" I insisted. They looked at each other doubtfully. Then at me.

Skinny. Wearing a plaid skirt and non-descript blouse. Ankle socks and oxford shoes.

"You shouldn't say things like that about men. You could get into a lot of trouble."

Angry and disappointed, I turned away. And there was Richie. Standing just outside the kitchen, in the hallway. He'd heard every word. A nasty smirk settled on his face. I pushed past him and went to my room, wishing I could lock the door behind me.

❖   ❖   ❖

The first person I decided to confide in outside of my family, was our neighbor, and my piano teacher, Zelda Sedgwick, or Mrs. S. I remember my mother once told me that Zelda had come to a party at our house. A party meant the kitchen table overflowing with twenty-sixers and forty pounders of rye, scotch, vodka and gin interspersed with drained beer bottles and overflowing ashtrays. Cigarette smoke wafted from room to room like mist on the Scottish highlands, and if Dad wasn't playing the guitar and singing, then Mom was squeezing the latest hits out of her accordion. People danced, or simply held each other up on the floor, depending on how late it was and how much liquor was left.

Into this schmozzle walks Zelda Sedgwick, long legged, horse-faced and easily six feet tall. Zelda's house boasted Axminster carpets, canaries in gilded cages, a piano the colour of ebony, and two pure bred spaniels. Her husband was a practical joker, a short little mustachioed dentist named Walter.

She walks in. "Hi, Edna!" she shouts over the din of the accordion, and spotting Dad sitting on a chair she marches over and plants herself right smack dab on his knee. Now, my father was a ladies' man, make no mistake. And he could sense out the subtlest flirt in the room and move right in. But a big woman who boldly threw herself into his arms even in fun, scared the living daylights out of him. He squirmed and blushed and didn't know *what* to do with his hands. Zelda found this side of Tommy wildly amusing. She took forever to get up again, enjoying every moment of Tommy's obvious discomfort.

That was my piano teacher, see. And I thought I could trust her. I mean, when I came into her house, into that white and green kitchen with the black and white squares of tile on the floor, sweet birdsong drifting on the air, and the promise of peanut butter cookies emanating from the oven, Mrs. S. herself pouring me a big tall glass of milk, and setting a plate in front of me, I felt I was in a sanctuary second only to heaven.

So I told her. Well, I sort of told her. But, Asperger me, I couldn't just come out and say Richie grabbed me and French kissed me. No. I felt it would be too unnerving for her to be broadsided with such brutally crude information. She had class and therefore I felt the need to approach the subject with some delicacy.

"How was school today?" she asked. I slipped my oxfords off under the table, using one foot to push the other shoe off, and swung my aching feet in the air under her table.

"Good. I read a poem I wrote in class and all the kids really liked it."

"Well, good for you! Did you bring it home so Mom and Dad could read it?"

I shook my head "no". "They don't read poetry, except the kind on greeting cards."

"Oh. Well, would you like to read it to me?"

I thought about my poem. It was about God and motorbikes. I didn't think Mrs. S. would take to it, exactly, her being Presbyterian.

"I left it at school," I lied. I didn't want to get into a discussion about my poem. I wanted to tell her what Richie did. "But something happened at Mom and Dad's party last weekend," I ventured.

Mrs. S. nodded and grinned. "Lots of things happen at your parent's parties. I hear things happening all night," she added.

"Well." I hesitated. Then sighed. How to couch this so that she would not be shocked? "What if I told you it was about Richie?"

"Oh, now that wouldn't surprise me. Not one bit," Mrs. S. said, a warm, happy look coming over her face. "He's a character, that one."

"What if I told you he French kissed me? Tongue and everything," I said, my face curling up as if I'd sucked a lemon.

I'll give her credit. At least she looked up from the tray of cookies she was pulling out of the oven. "You bad girl!" she said.

"No—" I said, about to say, *I didn't want to!*

But before I could, she went on, "You mustn't say things like that about men, even if you wish they were true," she began.

I scrambled to my feet, but what I'd meant to be a defiant stance and an indignant exit turned into me landing in a stumbling heap under the corner of the table as I tripped on my shoes and overturned my chair.

"Oh, no, you don't," she said, recognizing my aim of running out. Reaching for my arm, she hoisted me up with one hand while righting my chair with the other. "Now you sit down like a good little girl and eat those cookies."

Blinking back tears, I sat down with a rebellious thump. Mrs. S. eyed me somewhat sympathetically and said: "All girls think about boys. But Richie's married, and even if he wasn't, he's too old for you. You can understand that, can't you?"

I nodded miserably. Mrs. S. looked pleased. "Now you've got to promise never to repeat what you said." She eyed me grimly.

I looked away from her, down at the table, picking bits out of the buttery brown cookie she'd just put in front of me. Tears stung my eyes.

"But—Mrs. S," I began.

"Look at me, Margaret Jean," she demanded.

I raised my eyes to hers. "Stop blubbering and promise," she said firmly.

I sighed. What was the point of protesting? Anyway, what difference did it make? I blew out a huge sigh. "Okay, I promise."

She nodded, pleased. Until I added:

"Unless he does it again."

She gave me a sharp warning glance, and said, "Now you eat your cookie, and no more of your back talk, Miss."

I crumbled that cookie to smithereens. I refused to eat it. It would stick in my throat and choke me for sure.

❖ ❖ ❖

That was the great attraction that Frank de Courcy held for me, see. He was not the kind of guy any parent wants to find their thirteen year old daughter hanging out with that's for sure, and on the face of it, there was nothing good ever going to come out of my friendship with a juvenile delinquent from an up-Island Detention Home, but in my thirteenth year, I both feared and adored Frank. You couldn't have kept me away from him with a tow truck and a power winch. Because Frank believed me when I told him about Richie. He believed me and he was outraged.

And more than I needed Sunday School preaching or lessons in manners or a high school diploma, I needed Frank de Courcy to walk into my life and declare right out loud and with multiple curse words how wronged I had been, how screwed up my life was because of Richie, how candy-ass and nuts my family was not to believe me and how dreadful, how horrible, how bloody stinking awful it must have been for me. That was Frank and that summer of 1960, he was my savior.

Olive skinned, black haired, probably what my Grandmother would refer to as a 'half-breed', Frank was fresh out of Brannon Lake Reform School when I met him. He was a swaggering, swearing sixteen year old whose father had abandoned him and whose mother had named him "Bysshe" after the poet, Percy Bysshe Shelley. He renamed himself, and strode through life with a swagger, a switchblade in his boot, and a burning lust for revenge on the whole entire world. Only months after my abuser moved away to another part of Canada, Frank showed up on Eddy C's doorstep.

CHAPTER 12

Eddy was a couple of years older than I. He lived up a dusty path off Meaford Road, the road that ran behind ours, and fronted the abandoned gravel pit. I met him once or twice in the general neighborhood melee of backlot baseball and kick the can.

Eddy was home-schooled in the nicotine-stained kitchen where his mother sat in men's clothes and boots and nursed a coffee all day, rolling and lighting thin, misshaped cigarettes at close interludes.

I had this strange ritual I went through every time I left school to go to Eddy's. I would leave the school building, exiting down the main hall of Belmont High School and walking right through the gates as if I had permission to leave. It wasn't until I had walked along the flats up the hill past Hull's farm and veered right onto Station Road, past Anita Wood's house and come to the Meaford Road cutoff that I would stop.

I would stop and stand stock still, quiet my breathing, and close my eyes. Breathing deeply, I would concentrate on the blackness, and silently ask myself if I was going to get caught. If I felt only calmness and peace, I knew I wouldn't get caught. If I felt an inner excitement, what the Irish call "fey", I knew my parents would somehow find out that very day. If I felt that inner thrill or excitableness, I would just go home.

Mom worked, so she was never home. And Dad worked as much as his drinking allowed, so you might think I had nothing to fear. But if the phone rang, the school calling, and Grams had her hearing aid in, I was in for it. Big time. Strapped on the back of the legs. Not fun.

I did not see anything wrong in seizing this interlude, these brief hours of complete and utter peace. I felt exhausted from painfully maneuvering through the maze of social exchanges at school (or lack thereof), Maths that seemed like hieroglyphics to me, and the omnipresent sense of social inadequacy; so much so that it sometimes seemed impossible to survive another moment in the confines of the classroom. I think the most draining thing of all was always trying to put a good face on it. It was a relief to go to Eddy's.

Even now, just the physical image of him looming in the doorway, still comforts me. Naked to the waist and barefoot, his jeans too short and mended, blonde locks falling in his eyes, he'd smile shyly and invite me in.

It was really something, Eddy's house: two small bedrooms off a kitchen, walls yellow with nicotine, rooms steeped in the odor of stale tobacco and an overwhelming sense of the endurance of the human heart. A cast iron woodstove sat against the wall, and there was always an old-fashioned percolator coffee pot sitting on the back, the coffee pitch black and ready to pour.

The wall behind and to the right of the stove and another wall to the left of that boasted a wallpaper of ribbons and medals and badges Eddy had won for his rabbits and garden produce at different fairs. It was at once a humble house and a proud house, a place of abandonment and caring, a place for lost souls to gather and be gathered in.

Eddy had a nervous habit of always pushing his blond hair out of those dark eyes and he had a voice like brushed velvet. Even though he was older than me there was what seemed an aura of innocence about him and I always thought of him as a kid.

He once told me his family shame—that his father had sold his older sister, a tall willowy girl with striking looks—sent her out on the street to prostitute herself for their living. When his mom found out, she kicked the old man out of the house. Ever since, they'd subsisted on welfare and the hope that he'd die one day so they could collect on the life insurance.

Eddy told me one time seven years was up and they were about to go in and collect and the old man turned up on the doorstep just to thwart them. Eddy was the first person I ever knew that was home-schooled. He took courses by correspondence and was up to about grade eight when I met him. That was pretty much Eddy's life.

So I was skipping out on Math or something else I wasn't good at, and Mrs. C. told me Eddy wasn't home. His friend, Frank, just got out of the brig, and they were off downtown celebrating.

Disappointed, I turned to leave, but at the foot of the drive, I heard a holler and sure enough it was Eddy, hurrying over the fence and across the road to meet me, another kid in tow.

Only he wasn't a kid. You could tell that just looking at him. No matter his age, this guy had eyes as cold and hard as bedrock.

"Hey, Margaret," Eddy called. "Don't go. We just got here. C'mon, let's go up to the house." Eddy grinned with pride, looked back at his companion to see what he thought of me, and then burst into a knowing grin and led us back to the house.

Mrs. C. never got up. Eddy poured coffee into tin mugs for us, passing around tinned milk and sugar, and introduced me to Frank, his friend from Vancouver. I was wearing the orange and beige print skirt I had made in Home-Ec class with a crinoline and some rust coloured shoes with a bit of a heel. A beige sweater. I guess I looked prissy to Frank. Anyway he swore a lot just to see how I'd take it.

"How do you like these boots?" he asked, thrusting out a foot. I looked at them. They were black leather Wellingtons, complete with chains. All the rage. Expensive. "Now look at Eddy's," Frank said grinning with pride.

"Eddy! Where did you get them? They are really cool," I exclaimed.

Eddy laughed. "Frank ripped them off. Stole them right out in broad daylight. Some old lady was trying on every shoe in the store, and when the guy was in the back, Frank just picks them up and walks out the front door with the boxes under his arm."

"Walked around the corner," Frank added, "saw a bus and ran for it."

"Switched buses twice just in case," Eddy said. I could tell by the gleam in Eddy's eyes and the colour in his cheeks that he saw it as quite the adventure. I looked at Mrs. C. to see how she was taking it.

She just grunted out a laugh and pulled her tobacco pouch toward her, spilling an amount onto a cigarette paper on the table. In spite of her mannish clothes and her weather beaten look, I got the impression she had once been very beautiful. An elusive something in the elegance of her gestures, maybe, or maybe it was the mint condition 1951 Cadillac parked out front. That sort of vehicle tends to lend an air of elegance to just about anyone. It didn't run. After Eddy's Dad ran out on them, they couldn't afford the insurance, so it just sat out there, polished and gleaming among the dust and weeds like the remnant of a lost civilization.

Anyway, Frank reached in his jacket and pulled out a carton of cigarettes. "Here, Mrs. C. Save your fixin's." With a bit of a grand gesture he added, "I got 'em" he handed them to her, "just for you."

Tears filled her eyes. She blinked a bit above her weathered cheeks and nodded. "Players! Thank you, child," she said, scraping the tobacco back into her pouch, and taking up the blue carton. "That's real thoughtful of you."

"And I took care of Eddy, here, too. Can't be going around with your damned shoes fallin' apart.

Not if you're trying to make time with the ladies." Frank quirked a brow and gave me a look. The inference went right over my head.

"Eddy has a girlfriend?" I asked.

Frank kept his eyes on me. Seeing that I was serious he chuckled and said, "Guess not."

"Do you Eddy?" I asked. Eddy sighed, leaned his handsome head on his hand, looked up at me and said, "No. But I sure wished I did."

Eddy was such a sweet guy. My heart went right out to him.

CHAPTER 13

Sat. Aug 3, 1963.

Birnie overslept and Marg phoned him out of bed and he drove her and brought her home, around 1 p.m. She lunched & then slept most of afternoon. I did various. Marg to Devonshire[12] for supplies & Cora[13] sent six Zoonooz[14] via Steve M.

Saturday, August 3, 1963
Dear diary.

What a crazy day! Everything was upside down. You know, when it comes to this film business, mostly I feel like Cinderella. But not today.

Today it started out like Alice in Wonderland— down the chute and into the most unpredictable scenarios. It ended like Cinderella, though, me feeling like a princess—Damion O drove me home. And he kissed me.

I didn't look up to see if Grams was watching out the back door window. It wasn't till I got out of the car that I even thought of it.

Yours truly,

Margaret Jean.

Usually they sent a car and driver for me, but Bernie had to be on set and so he made arrangements to pick me up. Filming didn't usually start til around ten but set up—getting our marks, setting up the reflectors and equipment, started at eight a.m. on the dot. By seven-fifteen, I was ready; bathed, my hair brushed and pulled into a tight French roll, and I had slipped into the clothes laid out the night before. I'd even eaten the toast and grapefruit Grams had waiting for me.

By twenty after seven, I had applied fresh lipstick, checked my purse for tissues and money and stood watch at the front door window. Seven thirty and counting. I ducked into the biffy and out. Seven thirty five; no sign of Bernie. It was at least a fifteen minute drive to the shoot. Seven forty-five, I was pacing. Seven fifty—Grams came to tell me a watched pot never boils. Eight o'clock I was going out of my freaking mind, and I picked up the phone.

"Bernie?"

"Hullo?" Seriously sleepy voice.

"Bernie!! Aren't you up yet? We're supposed to *be* there by now!"

"Huh? Oh, Marg, oh shit! I'm sorry, I'll be ten minutes!"

Oh crap oh crap oh crap. We were late. We were going to be really, really late. Again I worried that we would get fired. Twelve minutes later, a cloud of dust announced Bernie's arrival. He whipped the sports car around the yard in a complete U-turn, hit the horn and threw open the door. I mouthed a kiss to Grams who waved a scarf to me, which I grabbed, and headed out the door.

Bernie drove like a fiend the whole way there, with the convertible top still down from the night before. Thank goodness Grams had given me that scarf. I wrapped it tight around my head and prayed that the speed wouldn't take all the pins out of my hair. And that we'd arrive safe. And get to keep our jobs.

We peeled into the parking lot half an hour late. I was very anxious about it, but, as soon as we got in, Bernie made apologies all round, totally taking responsibility, which not only seemed to placate everyone, but actually made Smith laugh.

Sometimes once a day starts out wrong, nothing goes right until the whole twenty-four hours is clocked out. Although it didn't seem that way at first. We did all the usual stuff—ran through our lines, then added the movements, and finally, broke for lunch.

After lunch, we got back to the set and no Smith. Usually he was waiting for us, but today, Smith was nowhere to be seen.

An hour went by. Finally, Damion looked at the camera and sound guys sitting on the sidelines smoking and talking and us actors standing around gabbing about nothing, and he stands up like he's come to a decision.

"Okay," he says, "let's run this scene."

The camera guy raises his eyebrows, and the sound guy rolls his cigarette around his mouth and grins, but they butt their cigarettes and put their headphones on, and Bernie and Tim and I scramble for our marks, and Damion calls "Take One".

Bernie opens his mouth to say his line when somebody bellows, "What the hell is going on here?" And in staggers Smith. He is stinko! Wow. He is like, drunk with a capital L-O-A-D-E-D. One thing about Dad, when he did drink? At least he could hold his liquor.

"I'm the director!" Smith announces, weaving on his feet. "Nothing happens on this set until I say so. Izzat clear?"

Damion tried to calm him down, but Smith resisted, shouting about how Damion was trying to take his job, demanding respect and making a huge fuss .

I moved away and looked out the window. Bernie stayed on his mark and stared at them the whole time; he thought it was hilarious. Tim just shrugged and studied the script for some play he's doing nights.

Finally, two of the behind the scenes guys helped Smith off the set. Bernie said afterwards they probably took him to a pub, but I heard later they took Mr. Smith to his hotel room to sleep it off.

Anyway, we shut down early, and Bernie offered to drive me home, but Damion wouldn't hear of it. He insisted on driving me himself. Which, at the time, seemed a little strange to me, but hey, he was the assistant director, right? I had to go with him. He held the door for me. I slid into the front seat beside him, and we drove in silence.

I knew Damion had lots to think about, and as for me, I was thinking how many times I've driven past all these places: Craigflower School, the Gorge, and the old manor house, and how different it all seems from the window of a sleek black car, coming home from a movie set.

The radio was on CBC, and the strange events of the day and the music, some symphony or etude, made everything seem surreal, like I was being chauffeured through a movie, a technicolor scene, sitting beside Damion in a vehicle that had the power to transport me to a whole new world.

In the car interior, I could smell the crisp, citified cleanness of Damion. My dad smells different, sort of old woolly pants and stale shirts, like they've hung in the closet forever. Damion's clothes smelled like the chemical they use in the dry cleaners and like his aftershave which wasn't Old Spice—something more subtle, musky but rich. His skin was white with coarse black stubble around his chin. Out of the corner of his eye he sees me looking at him and says, "I appreciate the silence. Not many kids your age are comfortable with that."

I shrugged.

What could I say? That I was used to drunks? Not in that way, of course. Dad just mostly went out and partied and came home at four or five or six a.m. And then Damion starting talking, telling me about Smith, about his life, and his drinking. "This is strictly between us," Damion said. I nodded.

We pulled into the long, dirt drive and for the first time I could see the little white bungalow as if were a thing apart from me, as if the very walls were not connected somehow to the pores in my skin, as if we had not suffered disappointments and betrayals, hardships and anxieties, trivial pleasures and fleeting triumphs within those very walls; as if the lilac bush outside my bedroom window had never seduced me with its scent, and the Virginia creeper with its vigorous red ripening had never hugged the womb-like walls of the room my brother Rob had shared with the washing machine and the freezer.

It seemed scant and small, and the shed behind it, with its untidy stacks of wood, old tires and conglomeration of buckets and garden equipment strewn about, sagged, as if someone had let the air out of it since I left that morning.

And my eyes encountered this with a shock, the same shock the body experiences diving into a glacier-fed lake into the bone-piercing chill of the water. With that same brutal suddenness, I saw that we are the "dirt poor", and there came with the realization a kind of pride in it, in all the sorrow and shame we had suffered, I had suffered, and I felt somehow ripe in it, and ready for whatever life might offer.

Damion leaned over, from what seemed a great maturity of manhood, and I felt the incompleteness of my youth, the uncertainty and unknown of everything beyond my years.

He cupped my face in his hand and gazed at me, as if I were of great interest to him, and I understood through the tension in his fingertips and the softening of his eyes that he saw me as a woman, not a child, and I smiled at him, this man beckoning me to join him in adulthood.

"I'd like to take you out," he said, not removing his hand. An assistant director, thirty-something, was making a date with me in the same language as the sixteen year old boy I dated, as if male desire was all one and the same, regardless of age or maturity, or status, as if there was only one universal language for it.

I had not expected an invitation, but if I had, I would have anticipated a more adult wording, something genteel and grown up. The shock of the everyday ordinary lameness of "I'd like to take you out" struck me, and Asperger me, I laughed, breaking the spell, and I nodded, and he said, "Tomorrow? Can I pick you up about ten?"

"No." I said. His hand came down, his eyebrows shot up, like no fledgling actress had ever said no to the dark-eyed, fair-complected young assistant director.

I could see it was a shock to his ego, his features set as if suddenly calcified, making him look even older which made me think he probably wore boxer shorts and I thought boxer shorts were square, effeminate, even.

"I have a date," I said.

"With who?" As if no-one else existed but Damion O.

"With Nick. Who do you think?"

"Can't you change it?"

"No. A bunch of us are going up to Port Renfrew. It's low tide, and there's going to be all sorts of botanical specimens. You know, starfish and things."

"Okay. How about next weekend?"

I thought for a minute about the heat of the day and the weirdness of it all and how Smith, a National Film Board director, someone I had hoped to idolize and revere was just a drunk like my dad, and how this man, this assistant director, who flew around the world to different work locations was sitting here, with me, in my hard-packed dirt drive, wanting to kiss me.

And I thought about Nick, the high-schoolness of him, the hugeness of his hands compared to his still burgeoning body and the hard slimness of him, the pleasure in his eyes when he saw me coming across a room.

Damion touched my face again, the brush of fingertips, an electric current sizzling under his touch, and suddenly I couldn't remember if I had any plans for next weekend or the next five years, so I said that should be fine. It should be fine.

I turned to leave, to remove myself from his field of attraction, to get clear away to where I could think and not be drawn by the gravitational pull of his desire, but he caught my arm. I turned toward him, and the intensity in his eyes affected my heart as if it was an instrument in the percussion section of a symphony.

I caught my breath and he drew me to him until I could feel his body heat, until I could feel the starchiness of his shirt, the stubble on his cheek. Fear and joy plundered through me, and I let him kiss me, let myself taste his lips, breathe in his scent, my heart syncopating to some strange new rhythm.

Then he drew back ever so slightly, and put his hands on my shoulders, and he would have kissed me again if I leaned ever so slightly forward. But I remembered Nick's blue eyes teasing me, Nick laughing, chasing me down the beach. And I didn't know where all this was going with Damion or even if I wanted it to go anywhere at all.

"Gotta run!" I said and slipped out of his arms and out of the car.

CHAPTER 14

August 4, 1963. Sunday.
Botanical Beach

    Can you believe I overslept? Went to Port Renfrew with Nick and etc. What a day. Exhausted. Will write more tomorrow.

    MJ

    Four thirty a.m.. Someone's banging on the back door. I am in my blue baby doll pyjamas, not exactly awake, when I remember: Nick! Botanical Beach! Oh crap I forgot to set my alarm! There is more pounding at the door and I hear Nick calling "Marg? Hey, Marg, Wake up!" I drag myself out of bed and open the door. Naturally Nick is standing there.

    The way his eyes sweep over me, reminds me my pj's are almost see-through. I cross my arms across my chest, and he grins. "Hi." He says. His eyes say a lot more than "hi".

"What time is it?" I ask.

"Get dressed."

"What time is it?"

"What difference does it make?" He bends down and kisses me, shoves me toward my room. "Hurry up. Gord's waiting."

I throw on my clothes; jeans, shoes, blouse, sweater, and dash to the door.

"You're wearing those shoes?" Nick asks incredulously, looking at my low-heeled pumps.

"What?"

"Go get your runners on." He gives me a shove toward my room.

Grams comes into the hallway. "Is everything alright?".

"I slept in, Grams. I'm going to Port Renfrew today, remember? Botanicals. Gotta change my shoes." I duck into my bedroom, kick off my pumps, dig around in my closet for my runners, find them and hobble back into the hall, one shoe off, one shoe on.

Grams blinks against the light. "You be careful dear," she says, looking vulnerable without her glasses, her blue nylon robe wrapped around her. I love that robe; it's made of imitation Swiss dot material, and is a perfect match with my baby dolls. Instead, Grams is wearing it over a long cotton nightgown.

"Shoes!" Nick points to my feet.

Outside, Gordy's truck engine idles; Gordy leans out the window and says, "Hey, you guys coming?"

I hop around on one foot getting my other shoe on.

"You can tie them in the car," Nick says.

"Don't trip, dear," Grams says, coming toward us. She kisses me on the cheek, the softness of her skin surprising.

"'Bye Grams, go back to sleep! See you later!"

And we are gone.

We drove for about an hour to get to our actual destination which was Botanical Beach, a shoreline south west of Victoria, renowned for its beauty and the variety of marine life found in intertidal pools that pock-mark the shoreline at low tide. I favored the purple sea urchins with their spiny "don't touch me" bristles, but all the sea creatures, the star fish, the anemones, even the crabs and clams seem to have a beauty of their own in this ocean-side wilderness.

The guys had a route all planned out, since Nick's friend Gord had come to do research for a paper he was doing in a University biology class.

He photographed different sites, and Nick made notes according to what Gord said about the different species and water temperatures and salinity. As for me, I just wanted to collect a few shells as mementoes of the day, but Nick said it was forbidden. "You have to leave everything just as we found it. Nothing comes into this area and nothing goes out."

We trekked for what seemed like hours, over shale and slate and sand, over barnacle beds and seaweed. By noon I was exhausted and starving, and realized I had left so suddenly, I'd forgotten to pack a lunch.

Nick grinned. "Oh, so you're hungry are you?" I nodded sheepishly.

"Do you like crab?" Gordy asked.

"Sure I love crab."

"Well, go catch one then," Gordy suggested.

"I'm just about hungry enough to do that!" I said.

Nick laughed and mussed my hair. "If you're nice to me I'll share my lunch with you."

"How nice?"

Nick grinned. "Eat first. Then we'll talk." He pulled a lunch sack out of his backpack and I saw that he had made enough for both of us.

"You packed a lunch for me!"

"No I didn't." I reached for a sandwich. He brushed my hand away. "That's mine. Yours are the ones with mustard." I laughed and tousled his hair.

It's funny how I came to be going steady with Nick. He wasn't one of the bad boys that I was so often drawn to, like the guys I'd known out of Oakalla Prison or the BC Pen or Brannon Lake Detention Centre. We met when I got my first acting role in the Drama Club at school.

My very first part made up for all the years of rejection. Miss Charles decided to do one scene from Shakespeare, the sleepwalking scene with Lady Macbeth's famous monologue, and I got to be that grand dame of theatre.

I reveled in it. Nick was stage manager at the time. He was a pretty typical kid, a bit shy, academically inclined, physically rugged, and religiously committed. He was also a couple of months younger than I was. None of this seemed to matter when I was with him.

He would come over to visit me, and find Dad sitting in the living room, reading the paper. "Hi, Mr. Adam," he'd say. Dad would lower his paper, nod, and go back to his paper. Nick would pick up the section Dad wasn't reading and settle into a chair, cross his legs and start reading.

They'd sit like that for twenty minutes, looking over the articles, reading whatever interested them. Sometimes they'd switch sections. Every now and then I'd hear the rustle of a page turning. Dad loved the sense of manly communion. As for me—it made me crazy!

CHAPTER 15

Diary, Esme Adam.
Mon. Aug. 5, 1963.

Mr. Ducouski[15] came for Marg & had others. She had dinner with officers of the Skeena[e]. Good shots of boat. I picked, washed & preserved blackberries with apples, nearly 4 qts.

The apple trees stretched their gnarled arms skyward in our front garden, and blackberries tangled in wild abundance under the red-barked Arbutus tree, between our house and our neighbour's rambling two-story pink shingled Cape Cod.

Soft, furry bunnies nested in tunnels that ran beneath the blackberry patches, but blackberry thorns are not to be underestimated. The painful certainty with which they pierce the flesh brings to

_____

e   The HMCS Skeena was a destroyer escort, built at Burrard Shipyards in Victoria, and launched in August 1952.

mind the Mother Goose rhyme about the man who jumped into a bramble bush and scratched out his eyes.

Every west-coaster knows to wear long-sleeves when approaching these bushes, and to toss a wide board in ahead to gain access into the briar patch, and its cache of rich ripe berries that swell in jeweled red and black clusters in the prickly undergrowth.

August 5, 1963. Monday.
Dear diary,

Tonight, we were invited, the cast and crew, to have dinner at the officer's mess on the ship. They were so frightfully correct. Damion was chastised for having his hand in his pocket.

Timothy kept imitating the officers when no-one was looking. It was wild! He had Bernie and I in stitches.

Damion tried to sit between me and Tim but the officers had a special place for him and old Smith, and a man in whites came and steered him to his reserved seat. It was better anyway: Bernie and Tim were lots of fun.——And I could flirt with Damion across the table.

Margaret Jean

The dining table seemed vast, and Damion a sea of white linen away, though whenever I paused to look in his direction, his eyes met mine. The officers looked as if they came in a set, neatly boxed, all made from the same mold. Shaved, short-haired, capped, uniformed, they presented just that—a uniform gathering. I had two previous contacts with the military: Richie, a pervert who rented our cabin before Maria moved in, a complete creep, and the extreme opposite, Carson Andrews, an ordinary seaman who was a friend of a friend in Oak Bay.

Carson was just a sailor, not an officer—a nineteen year-old boy I knew in the trauma of my thirteenth year when I still inexplicably woke every day with the fear of Richie. Richie who was gone, transferred back east.

Dear, strong, capable Carson. He was a lean six foot two, and seemed a very adult nineteen, drinking hard whiskey and driving an old high horse-power Indian motorcycle with a lot of chrome.

Carson's black hair was shaved so short the curl showed only in the close-cropped wave of it, and I liked how he smelled. He had what I considered a manly scent, vestiges of leather and gas fumes and cigarette smoke and the soap-clean smell of his skin, all over-laid with the scent of Blue Velvet Cologne.

Those Sunday nights he drove me home from Cheryl's place in Oak Bay, both of us rode the chrome and leather and fumes of his Indian as if nothing could touch us once we were in motion, as if we could ride out the future together.

These officers in training were nothing like that. They were stiff and precise, and it was the absolute perfection of them, the white gloves, the overly correct etiquette, the erect posture, the perfectly controlled setting—white linens glittering with polished silver and crystal glasses—and in the midst of it all, me, feeling very hot and sticky and out of place, and wishing for Carson Andrews and the wind in my hair, or Nick chasing me down the beach, catching me, and then, that softness in his eyes just before he kisses me.

CHAPTER 16

Midnight. Monday again.

Grams came and rapped softly at my door and told me Mom and Dad are coming home tomorrow. She said it like I would be glad. I suppose I should be, but how? How can I be glad?

Yours truly,

Margaret Jean.

The truth was, during the day when I was helping Grams look after the younger kids, when I was taking up the slack in the housework, vacuuming, mopping, dusting and canning fruit, during the day I was not allowed out of the yard. The rare exception occurred when we needed something at the store.

In those days, it was not like it is for many people now. You didn't just go to the store to hang out or to buy something like a slushy or a pizza. In our family, we shopped for groceries once every two weeks—on payday I guess. And what we got had to last.

But on those rare occasions when Grams made up her mind to make something special and we didn't have an ingredient for it, she'd send me to Price's Store. Not Cooper's, because we didn't have an account there—the kind of account that pre-dated credit cards. No, it was always Price's store, that big white-sided general store where Mr. & Mrs. Price presided, or occasionally their daughter, Maureen, might be at the till taking cash.

Needless to say, I was always delighted when Grams discovered a lack that would send me, note in hand, off to the store. But even there, my parents had strict limitations.

For instance, I could not walk the three or four blocks further along the highway to the Devonshire Store and Pool Hall. That was definitely out of bounds. And there was always a time limit—if it took me half an hour to walk to the corner, get what I came for and return home, I would be greeted with, "What took so long?" There was no time for idle chatter or just day-dreamy browsing around.

Thus, getting on a bus and riding into downtown Victoria for a film audition was a very daring thing for me to do. And then getting a job where cars driven by absolute strangers came and picked me up and whisked me off into unknown parts of the city, I knew that was incomprehensible to my parents. And I could not think exactly how they would react, or what implications their reaction would have for me.

Darkness pervaded my relationship with my parents and their relationship with each other, casting a dark pall over our family life.

My father worked hard to keep us afloat, but he'd left the army without any particular skills. Carpentry, fire-fighting and even grave digging kept us going, while Mom worked in the laundry or cleaning hotel rooms, and Grams contributed what little she could from her pensions.

In our family history, debt was a common denominator. My paternal great grandfather borrowed money against crops, land and oxen to save his farm and obtain the government position that he lobbied to create, and then died young, leaving his wife no choice but to return to her sisters in California.

Our debt was not imbued with the promise of improvement, and my father did not die until the age of eighty-seven.

In those early days, he liked to celebrate without us, on drunken rampages, finding parties and fist fights, until sometime in the summer of 1959, a year after Richie and Andrea moved out, when he and Maria decided they'd had enough booze and joined Alcoholics Anonymous together at 4 a.m. At that time, Maria lived with her husband, Doug and two dogs in the rental cabin on our property so Dad couldn't really sneak home without Maria.

Some people said Dad stayed out so late with her because he was just too scared to come home with another woman, but they didn't know Dad. It wouldn't have been fear, but his sense of propriety.

Besides, none of that had ever inspired him to quit drinking before. Looking back, I think Dad must have had one of those moments of clarity in which he found himself grave-digging in the muck and the rain, his life dissipating in the most menial labour.

Or perhaps Maria inspired their sobriety, who knows? Drinking, my father was a menace, but for the first ten years at least, sober, Dad was a self-righteous, angry, disappointed and demanding man. When I was sixteen, he had been unbearably sober for three years.

Sobriety also didn't change the fact that he wasn't where or what he wanted to be. While he wanted Mom and us kids at home, he had little interest in us.

I sang in choirs that entered provincial competitions, acted in plays, was on sports teams for years, but with one exception, he did not come to my games, concerts or plays.

The exception was when I was in grade four. It was sports day and we had many competitions; foot races, high jump, long jump, relays. I participated in all, and won the silver trophy for my grade. By the time it was awarded to me, it had a number of dark fingerprints on it. Sitting in the stands with Dad, I took out my hanky and started to polish the fingerprints away. I suppose it took quite some time, because Dad said, "Put that away."

"I'm cleaning it," I said.

"No-one else is cleaning their trophy," Dad said, his face red with embarrassment.

I stopped, but Dad had been shamed by my behavior, and he never attended any event I partook of after that. Once again, my Asperger's behavior, my complete oblivion to what anyone else was doing, or how everyone else was behaving, severed a tenuous connection with my parent.

Or maybe it was the fact that he was the only father there, that he was unemployed, and thus able to attend, while his wife was working, and couldn't. Maybe that was the real shame of it. Whatever the reason, Dad's embarrassment left me with a sense of that sudden severing of a precious connection between my father and myself; one I valued, one I thought I had finally succeeded in making.

Probably it was the latter, his unemployment, that made him swear off our extra-curricular activities. Because things didn't change for Scott either. Mom was the one who played catch with him, who drove him to practices, who, when she wasn't working, showed up at his games.

It always felt to me like Dad longed for someone else's company; as if he was painfully confined within our family, irritable and displeased because none of us were the people he wished to have around him. I suppose this scarcity of love, this lack of affectionate welcome or cheerfully shared pastimes was somehow converted in my mind into financial poverty.

In truth, we lived an abundant life. Peach, apple and pear trees grew on our property, and that fruit was harvested and stored for winter. Our vegetable garden provided all the lettuce, beets, carrots, onions, marrows, squashes and beans that anyone could want. The excess lettuce went to the chickens and rabbits; the beets, and beans were preserved, the carrots, potatoes, marrows and squashes were stored in the root cellar, a spidery darkness dug out beneath the house. And every fall my parents--in fact all of us, participated. We slaughtered, plucked and froze any hens that weren't laying.

One of my most vivid childhood memories is the blood-stained chopping block, my father towering over it, an axe in one fist, and a fowl grasped by its scaly yellow legs in the other. With an easy dexterity he'd lay the squawking, fluttering, frantic bird's head on the block, and in that one moment when the chicken was still enough, my father would swing the axe with frightening efficiency, separating head from body. With one deft swipe he'd sweep the beady-eyed head aside, dropping it, beak gawking open in its final silent scream, to the ground.

And then he'd toss the chicken's body to the other side. And then, a most unsettling, mortifying exhibition; sometimes the headless chicken would right itself, stand up and run headless around the yard in a brief instinctive attempt to flee, running blindly in crazy circles bumping into Dad and the chopping block, tripping over its own head, running frantically until all the blood had spurted out of its body and then--it just flopped over dead.

The first time this happened? Asperger me, I laughed. It was paradoxical to see a dead thing, headless, scrambling frantically to escape the tragic end that had already befallen it. Nightmarish.

Ghoulish. So incredibly *paradoxical* that it struck me as hilarious. And absolutely terrifying.

Adding to the terror was the fact, which didn't escape me, that my father, who lashed me with a belt, who fought my big brother, Rob with his fists, was damn good with that axe.

During one session of butchering the chickens, dad actually started talking to me about the process, a rarity in our family. He said a Jewish man in the army told him a different way of killing the hens; first, string the live chickens upside down, then cut the carotid artery and let them bleed out. Dad thought the axe brought a swifter, more humane demise.

Anyway, once the chickens were lying on the ground, without moving, my brother and I would pick up the birds, still warm and sticky, and bring them to Mom or Grams, who oversaw huge tin tubs of boiling hot water.

The birds were dipped into the water, to release the pinfeathers, then hung up by their scrawny yellow feet on the side of the chicken shed. Standing below, we plucked all the feathers, after which they were gutted, washed in clean water and wrapped and frozen.

At the end of the day, our arms and necks and backs ached, and we stunk with the smell of sweat and blood. I ran for the bath before anyone could stop me, and plunged into a hot tub, scrubbing hard and doing my best to get out before anyone came in the house to use the bathroom and started pounding on the door.

Meanwhile, Mom and Grams and any help that were currently living in, prepared heaping pans of fried chicken to reward us. We ate with relish.

Girls, often cousins from Saskatchewan, or the daughters of families that lived in more rural areas, came to stay with us and work in the house. They were often skittish about chicken-plucking, preferring to cook, sew and babysit.

And of course, there was the cabin, painted Bark Brown or Indian Red as it was called in those days, with turquoise trim. Erected by Dad and friends of the family, it was a simple four room structure; two bedrooms, a combined kitchen/living room and a single bath, and it must have provided an additional income stream for the family, before the Legion bought us out and they tore the old house and outbuildings down. The cabin was always rented.

But my childhood memories are awash in impoverishment, and I always thought the sense of deprivation was all about the money we didn't have. But when I look back on the gardens, the rental cabin, the chickens and rabbits that we raised, the side of beef that was bought, cut, wrapped and frozen every fall, I realize it was not financial poverty that crippled us. It was an impoverishment of spirit.

When Mom and Dad were gone, the house seemed light and airy; like a place where dreams could come true, where one could exercise control and find their true path in life. Where God and the Holy Spirit beamed in on sunlit dust motes.

But when my parents were present, everything became muddied again. A heaviness settled, suffocating, draining, exhausting me, and I was unable to pinpoint the source, to discover why and how it all changed when Mom and Dad came home.

Gram's announcement caught me by surprise. Of course, I'd known they had to come home sometime. I was just hoping it would be more distant. I stopped staring at the ceiling and rolled over and went back to sleep.

CHAPTER 17

Tues. Aug. 6, 1963.

Did up the ironing AM & etc. Edna & Tommy returned about 4 PM   Marg worked, she & Nicky out eve.   Union phoned. Work for Tommy to-morrow.

August 6, 1963. Tuesday.

Well, things on the set went just fine for once.   Mom and Dad and the kids came home today.   Mom and Dad didn't say much about the movie.   Dad just laughed and shook his head when I told him about it, and said, "Is that right?" like he couldn't believe it.   And Mom just said I'd better not think I was going to get out of my chores because of being in a movie.

Scott is glad to be back, playing with his Tonka trucks and lassoing and tying up the neighbor kids.   Terry gave me a big hug when I came home, and showed me where

*she fell and scraped her knee. I watched her play 'go fish'
with Scott & Graham until Nick came.*

Yours truly,
Margaret Jean.

"Margy, why does the dealer always win?"
Scott asked. Scott and his friend, Graham looked
annoyed.

"They don't."

"And how come the dealer gets to see everybody's cards?" Graham added.

I laughed. Trust Terry. "Oh well, next hand,
you'll be the dealer," I said.

"No. Terry's *always* the dealer." Scott said,
throwing his cards in.

"Terry!" I said. She looked at me, *Just stay out
this, Sis.*

Just then Nick came, and as I grabbed my
purse, I heard her say, "Those *are* the rules." And
the sound of cards hitting the table.

Weds. Aug. 7, 1963.

*Tommy to work. Edna to town. Marg worked & had
supper on location. Eve, Tommy drove Jillian and Marg
to bowl. Wrote Nell and sent her discharge papers. 3 letters today.*

❖   ❖   ❖

In spite of the early morning mists, we set up in Beacon Hill Park beside the duck pond. I'm feeding the ducks and Tim is with me, and we're talking about how unhappy he is. I'm kneeling throughout the whole scene, only I'm not kneeling exactly, I'm crouching beside the duck pond, feeding the ducks. I'm in position so that the crew can set up the reflectors and cameras. It takes awhile to get things in position, but when they're ready to shoot, the weather won't co-operate. One minute it's cloudy and the next, sunny. And sometimes the clouds move in front of the sun, and we have to wait some more. At first my legs are killing me, all scrunched up like they are, but after awhile my feet and legs go numb. Finally, the light is just right, and we start the shoot, but it turns out the ducks are all on the other side of the pond, so Smith decides to give them a few minutes to come back.

The crew breaks for a cigarette and coffee and that done with, we clue into the fact that the ducks are not coming back of their own free will. Since it's definitely too much work to move the set-up, Damion and some of the guys sit on the edge of the pond cooing and calling, trying to get the birds to come back. But by this time, the ducks are fast asleep. Just like my legs.

Smith insists we need the birds to make the scene work, and sends some of the crew around to chase the ducks out of the reeds. The ducks are annoyed at being disturbed, and just flap around and settle back down in the same place. After a few attempts it becomes clear these ducks have no intention of coming back to our side of the pond. During this considerable time, I am still uncomfortably crouched, waiting, in the hot glare of the reflectors.

It is all futile until finally, Damion runs to a nearby grocer and buys a whole bag of bread crumbs. He gets down beside me, and heaves the whole lot into the water. The ducks see the bread and go nuts. They come racing back, clambering over each other, half flying, half swimming and pecking madly at the bread. We start shooting the scene. It's a few takes before it's exactly right and Smith says "Cut" and everyone starts to leave.

Except me. By now, I can't stand up. After being crouched all that time in a kneeling position, I have no feeling left in my legs. I can't get up. In fact, I think that the only thing I can do is fall over.

Damion sees me and comes over. "You coming?" he asks.

I blush. "I can't move."

He looks mortified, then laughs, and gives me his hand. "You should have said something!"

He helps me up, his arm around me, lifting me. I am intensely aware that his body is not like

Nick's; that it is thicker somehow, though not fat at all, and I am sensitive to my own awareness of the flesh that lies under his shirt. He holds me, casually, his arm around my waist, until the pins and needles and prickles are gone. He doesn't wear Old Spice, but whatever it is, it makes me think of nude bodies tangled in perfumed sheets in the dark.

After lunch, we're ready to film another scene in the park. My line is "What's the matter, Tim?"

I ask it sympathetically. Damion is upset. I'm supposed to be angry.

"My boyfriend has a problem and I'm going to yell at him?" I ask. "Why would I do that?" Damion is frustrated, and I'm feeling like he thinks I'm weird or something.

When it's time to shoot the scene, the cameraman points out that my nose is sunburned. "Go and put some more foundation on," Smith advises.

"Foundation? I never wear foundation."

Smith blew. "Why didn't anybody recognize this fact before now?" he asks, waving his script.

The cameraman shrugs. "You can't tell. Look at her skin--it's flawless."

Now that's a compliment.

❖ ❖ ❖

UNFORGIVING

August 7, 1963, Wednesday.
Dear Diary,

How strange this filming business is. Not glamorous like I thought in the beginning. Smith says I have to wear foundation. Ugh!

Anyway, after we finished shooting, Damion said he'd drive me home. Sydowski and Smith kind of looked at him, but they said okay

We headed out and Damion asked if I wanted to have dinner with him at the new White Spot, up by the new Town & Country Shopping Centre. After, he wanted to go somewhere and park, but I nixed that. I had other plans.

When we drove in, Dad came out and stood on the porch. I introduced him to Damion, and when he shook hands with Dad, Dad got this funny little grin on his face, like "I know the kind of guy you are, alright." And a little laugh escaped his lips.

I blushed, remembering how soft Damion's hands are.

Damion looked him straight in the eye. Dad didn't faze him one bit.

Anyway, tomorrow I have to find time to buy foundation. Cover Girl, I guess. Smith says I have to wear it for the rest of the film. If only he knew how much it gunks up your pores he wouldn't dream of asking me to do that. All those years of Noxzema face wash and Max Factor cold cream right down the drain.

Yours truly,
Margaret Jean.

Thurs. Aug. 8, 1963
Tommy's 49th Birthday.

Rested a lot & had hair done at Colwood. Edna washed & did kitchen floor. Marg & Tommy worked. Cora & Steve Miller wrote asking me to go stay awhile there.

August 8th, 1963. Dad's birthday.

Well dear diary, another day at work. Damion kept telling me to stand up straight, and jabbing me between the shoulders. That works. Nothing spectacular happened. Dad's birthday today. He's a Leo. The lion. Fire is his element and the Sun rules him. Now me, I'm a Virgo. Earth is my element, and Mercury rules me. Mercury, mercurial. Is that me? Dad's more likely to lose his temper. What about Mom? She's a Cancer. A crab. (giggle). Mom might be okay if she wasn't so sad all the time. If she had a little life in her. Gotta go. They're shooting at six tomorrow. A.M.!

Margaret Jean.

There is no mention of any celebration of my father's birthday: there is no mention of a birthday cake, or cards exchanged, or gifts. Looking back, I wonder how my father felt about the lack of recognition. But then, we seldom celebrated birthdays. I can only remember one birthday party for myself, and none for my older brother. I don't even remember celebrating my grandmother's, mother's, or father's birthdays.

It's a strange thing, in retrospect, this lack of celebration of one's birth, one's beginnings, the lack of joy over another year conquered, enjoyed, embraced. And I did the same with my children and myself as an adult. Only since marrying Chris has there been notice taken of special days. And even then, perhaps not enough notice. Amazing the patterning we accept, imprint and pass on.

Fri. Aug. 9, 1963.

Tommy & Marg worked. Edna baked bread & ironed. I picked blackberries & apples & made 5 ½ qts. Preserves. Wrote Cora, also Luke & Ethel. Marg & Nicky out eve. Henrys here eve.

Mom had a wonderful talent for bread baking. Every two weeks she would make up a batch of yeast dough that provided a dozen loaves of bread and at least two dozen buns; crisp-crusted, caramel colored buns with smooth white innards. Our favorite thing (and Maria's—she always turned up on baking day) was to break one open releasing the warm, yeasty aroma of fresh-baked bread, and slather both halves with butter. It was Maria's favorite treat, and even after she was divorced and moved away out of the cabin, she'd drive over and sit shamelessly at our table, her earrings dangling to and fro as she chewed. She said she had "baking day radar"; and would just show up, acting out her role of family friend.

I don't remember Mom having any particular response to Maria. She seemed glad enough to see her, and it used to irk us kids; even Scotty at age six knew perfectly well what was going on. Mom seemed the only one oblivious. In later life, I learned that Dad had other affairs. Some before I was born. Her attitude with Maria is hard to peg down; it was not one of stoic resolve. Nor did she fight the affair. I think it can best be described as one of resignation. Or maybe she was relieved that someone else was taking the brunt of the wifely duties. The only thing my mother ever told me about sex was that it was "messy", a word she issued with a particularly sour expression.

And of course, she would always be "putting on a good face" for us kids, behaving as if nothing was wrong so as not to upset us. It worked quite the opposite. We wanted her to express the outrage we all felt and oust Maria and establish herself as our family matriarch. Instead, she listened to Grams who was always telling us to cheer up and make the best of things, Mom giving the impression of a martyr, someone too weak to hold her own against the brazen Maria let alone our stalwart and dignified grandmother.

Oddly enough, Maria used to stick up for Mom if Dad was around and talked down to her. "Don't let him get away with that, Edna!" she'd admonish Mom. She'd give a throaty laugh, and tell Dad, "It's a good thing you're not married to me!"

CHAPTER 18

August 9, 1963. Friday.
Dear Diary.

Nick was very upset today because I'm going to the Beach Party with Jillian instead of him. He actually got tears in his eyes and his nose went all red. All six feet of him turned into this big soft noodle of guy, and I couldn't stand it. I've never seen him like that before. Jillian said it would make her go all soft inside; he really loves you, Marg. But I hated him like that.

Yours truly,
Margaret Jean

Jillian's father was a retailer; her Mom and Dad owned and worked in the little shop on Douglas Street in downtown Victoria. Her mother wore dark hair pulled straight back off the fine bones of her face. Both Jillian's parents were slight, short people, but Jillian in her teens, was tall and big-boned, with what was for her, an annoying birthmark on her knee. She had lovely eyes, a soft, pleasant voice, and a way of laughing that was like releasing a gush of happy sound. Easy-going and giggly, Jillian was a fun friend. We used to sing whenever we were together; sometimes hymns from the little brown Baptist Church we both attended on Sundays, sometimes songs from the current hit parade. Sometimes we'd just walk to the Devonshire, a little corner store about a block from Jillian's house, and have a coke.

When I met an old school acquaintance, Leslie Edwards, again forty years later, she remembered Jillian. "We were having a sleep over and we both had these cute little baby doll pyjamas on. Jillian was set on Dalton DesRocher, you remember him, and he was at the pool hall down the end of Jillian's road, playing pool. So we got this idea to run down there see, and run around the pool hall in our baby doll pyjamas. So we did." Everyone at our table looked at Leslie in awe.

"You did that? You really did?" I asked.

"Of course we did," Leslie replied, "But nobody looked up! They never even saw us."

"How very disappointing," Don said.

Leslie had a sip of her drink, and added, "So we had to go round again."

We all collapsed with laughter.

Jillian was the perfect companion for the beach party.

❖   ❖   ❖

We sat in the driveway in the old Hudson, Nick with his arms wrapped around the steering wheel, his chin resting on the top curve.

"So I won't get to see you tomorrow."   He lifted his head and said, "I never get to see you anymore," His body was muscular and lean under his tee shirt and jeans. I liked the look of him, the curve of his arms, the thick slash of his lips. The leanness of his hips.

"That's just silly!" I protested. "We've been out tonight, haven't we? And we spent all day Sunday together, and we went out Tuesday night. I mean, Geez."

He sat up, tapped the steering wheel with his fist, and said "So what are you doing tomorrow?"

"It's work, really," I lied. "You know—it's the beach party, for the cast and crew."

"So—just ask if I can come, then. They know me—it'll be cool." He reached over to draw me into his arms, all smiles and thinking everything was fine between us.

I backed myself up against the passenger door. "But I promised Jillian, Nick. And she's really excited about meeting a producer and director and all."

Nick's eyes got dull. He pulled back. "So what's really going on."

"Nothing." It wasn't true and we both knew it. I sensed in Damion an escape route, the possibility of a different life, one far removed from Langford and Colwood and chicken plucking and baby-sitting. A glamourous life, traveling the world, doing things I wanted to do, being who I wanted to be. I had to be with Damion at the party, and if Nick came, that wouldn't happen. Damion had promised to introduce me to some theatre people here in Victoria and I wanted that intro. I loved Nick, not Damion. But the filming would be over in a couple of weeks at most, and then Nick and I could get back to normal. He could wait til then. I glanced up at him.

To my surprise, tears had welled up in his eyes. His nose, a rather prominent feature in his face, got red. *Nick was crying*.

I'd never seen a man cry before. Not ever. And now, here was Nicholas, six foot two, the man I had thought would protect me against all evil for the rest of my life, here he was, folding, crying, breaking down over a silly stupid thing like a *date*.

Suddenly, I couldn't stand him. I flew out of the car, and ran into the house, slamming the door behind me. Disappointment left a sour taste in my mouth, a cramping fear in my gut. I was alone again. The one person I thought I could depend on to protect me from all other men was obviously not man enough to do the job.

❖   ❖   ❖

It was what happened with Richie that made it impossible for me to love Nick any longer. Even though it happened four years before, even though it had nothing to do with Nick, it reached out like a monstrous tentacle over time and ripped me away from him.

CHAPTER 19

Pervert that he was, Richie waited a few weeks after the French-kissing episode. I guess he was taking his time, making sure no one believed me. He hadn't made any further overtures, and when I told a friend at school she laughed at me.

"You just made that up," she said.

When I protested, she added, "Those army boys get all the nooky they want from real women."

I kicked a pebble on the pavement and figured out right then and there, no one is ever going to believe me.

Life went on as usual, and other than my annoyance at not being believed, I pretty much forgot the whole thing.

Until I went to Aunt Nell and Uncle Ralph's big pink shingle house one night. I was looking after my cousins while Ralph and Nell went for a few beer. They met Dad at their usual haunt, the Six

Mile House. Mom was home, probably crocheting or resting, and Andrea, too.

But Richie just happened to drop in to the pub. Seeing Dad, he went over to sit in with them. After a bit he probably said something innocuous to Nell like, "So you're out and about. Who's home minding the kiddies?"

Nell wouldn't have thought twice about the question. No alarm bells went off. She assumed Richie was just making conversation. After all, perverts don't wear big signs on their foreheads. They don't have digital read-outs flashing from their person. No identifying badges. So he was just a married man, her brother's tenant, and she felt she knew him well enough to say, "Oh, Tommy dropped Margy off."

A normal conversation between friends. Who would have thought otherwise? And when Richie made his excuses and left early, no-one thought anything of it, except that maybe he was finally going home to Andrea. Andrea who was painting another coat of polish on her nails, glancing at the clock from time to time as he drove past the Station Road cabin, on to Sooke Road and turned left on Happy Valley, driving in the moonlight until he turned into the drive of my aunt's two-story house.

The sound of his engine brought me to the window. Richie's car?! I was frozen by fear, I couldn't even say why. I only knew I was suddenly praying "God, oh God, make him go away, please make him go away!!". Instinctively, I dashed from door to door, turning the locks, flicking out the porch light as I fled by, fear a fire licking my fingertips. Stumbling in my haste, I tore down the steep cellar stairs, to the ground level basement, feet tingling, hands trembling as I turned the lock against him, eyes wide, heart pounding as he tried the door, shaking the lock, turning, twisting and rattling the knob.

"Margy, Mar-gee?" I hate that name.

"Margy? Open the door. Margy!"

I fled in silent prayer to the top floor, into the corner of the dining room, in behind the curtains, swaddling myself in their comforting folds, praying, "Oh Lord Jesus, please, please make him go away." I stood trembling, my body sick and weak with fear. The harsh sound of my breathing echoed in the darkness.

He approached the front door. "It's better if you open the door, Margy. I can and will come in."

My heart pounded in my chest. Hammered in my ears.

The door knob rattled. I held my breath. "Thank you, thank you, thank you, God," I whispered as the lock held. I heard the tap, tap, tap of his footsteps on the porch steps. The slam of the car door. An engine firing. The sudden flicker of light in the room meant he had turned the headlights on. He was leaving! I breathed another prayer of thanks on a sigh of relief.

Relief which flooded through me, washing out all strength and will before it. Emboldened by his failure, I stepped out from behind the curtains. Weak and trembling, I tip-toed to the edge of the window careful to stay out of sight. I had to see him leave.

But to my dismay, the headlights were suddenly extinguished. The engine cut. Richie sprang out of the car and strode purposefully toward the garage. My knees buckled. The garage was separate from the house. What on earth was he doing in there?

My stomach cramped, my feet froze. My hands were cold and drenched with sweat. I had no idea what Richie was doing, I only knew it couldn't be good. I stood, riveted to the floor, trying to think.

In those days there was no 911, no child help lines. My parents were his friends and like my aunts and my friends would never believe Richie capable of what my mind instinctively knew he was capable of—unspeakable behaviour. And it was termed 'unspeakable' because even if and when it was happening to you, it was unmentionable. It was never a topic of conversation.

Even so, my aunt and uncle—what would they do? They wouldn't believe me over him, I felt certain of that. So I just stood at the window, my heart trying to beat its way out of my flat chest, my breathing fast and shallow.

I was eleven years old, I could not move, I could only stand frozen by the window and wonder what on earth he was doing.

Where exactly was he? "Oh God, Oh Jesus, help me," I whispered.

It was not a curse, but a direct and earnest address. And wonder as I would, I could not come up with any semblance of an idea of what Richie was doing out there. My mind was completely blank, a black bottomless pit of numbing fear imprinted with the image of Richie going into the garage and nothing else.

And then, a door swung open.

In my mind's eye I saw with sudden clarity, the tiny second-story balcony; just big enough for a person with a laundry basket. I saw it in such incredible detail; the reel that the blue clothesline ran around; the wooden pegs with the wire springs stored in a musty old flour sack with a drawstring rim. The dirty old dog mat draped over the railing. And the one door that didn't lock.

Richie must have seen it when he scouted the house, and when he saw the garage in the head-lights, he recognized a way of getting from the garage roof onto the clothes porch. I wanted to faint, to lose consciousness, but I could only stand as if in some invisible torture chamber, perspira-tion running rivulets down my body.

A light flicked on. Richie stood grinning across the room, red curls damp with sweat, a creepy grin breaking up his freckles. "I brought you some-thing" he said, thrusting a chocolate bar at me. I looked at it, unable to move, to reach for it, to push it away.

He pocketed it, approaching me, step by step. I stood, trapped in my own fear, unable to break free, to smash through or overcome my paralysis in any way. Like a rabbit facing a snake, I could barely breathe, let alone fight him off.

He didn't rape me. There was no penetration. But I was violated and humiliated. In my mind, I had been raped. I was furious and helpless.

When he was done, he said, "They won't believe you about this, either. So let's just keep it between us. When we're married, we'll have to do this often."

Somehow that statement in its total and absolute absurdity broke the horrid spell I'd been under.

"Married! You're married already. With children!"

"Andrea and I are getting divorced." He lit a cigarette, drew deeply on it, and said, "You know what that means, don't you? We're engaged." And he laughed as if it was such a joke; tossed the chocolate bar on the table and left.

I remember that I didn't cry. It would be giving in to cry.

CHAPTER 20

Frank, that hard-assed sixteen year old man-boy told me I looked eleven. "I'm thirteen," I said, embarrassed and insulted.

"Come here, then," he said. "And let me take a good look at you."

"You can see me just fine from there." We were out in the field behind Eddy's place, in the flats before the steep decline into the gravel pit.

"You chicken?" he asked.

"About what?"

"Come here."

I looked over at Eddy. He was chewing a piece of grass and trying to look nonchalant, avoiding my gaze. And suddenly an urge overwhelmed me.

"Why don't you come here?" I asked. I was flirting. It was dangerous and I knew it, but I couldn't help myself. I was pretty sure I had Frank figured out to be completely harmless to me, and I was testing my theory. But I was scared, too, and trying not to show it. I realized I was counting, heavily counting on Eddy coming to assist me if anything should get out of hand. After all, Eddy himself had never laid a hand on me.

Frank grinned, then strolled over to me. He got uncomfortably close but I held my ground. He looked me up and down and I slapped him hard. He caught my hand and laughed.

"Whoo, she's got a temper. You didn't tell me, Eddy, you didn't tell me she had a temper."

Our eyes locked. A thrill of terror ran through me, terror and joy, a feeling unlike any other I had ever experienced. And then he released my hand.

"I didn't hurt you. Why'd you hit me?" his voice was hard like steel, and quiet.

"It seemed like a good idea at the time." I said.

"You got good instincts, kid."

"Too bad I developed them so late in life," I said.

He eyed me quizzically for a long minute. Then: "Somebody bothering you?" he asked.

"Not anymore." I said.

"When?"

"When I was just a kid. Eleven. Twelve." Something in me screamed that I was never a kid. But I just spoke in normal tones. As if we were talking about what we had for lunch. It didn't fool Frank.

"Tell me who."

"What difference does it make now?"

"Tell me, and I'll kill the bastard."

I looked at him to gauge his meaning. I stared at him. Then I said, "You're kidding, right?"

He had backed away from me and his hands were by his sides and I saw that they were shaking, that he was trembling with rage, and suddenly my world came undone.

All the frozenness inside of me, the pent up anger stacked up inside me like a mountain-range of glaciers piled atop a sea of ice bergs, that impenetrable core I had developed, the cold and bitter lie that kept me safe, the lie that I was Okay, that none of it mattered, that protective wall was suddenly shattered, breaking up and heaving, melting in a sea of passion and emotion.

Someone believed me. Someone acknowledged me. Someone finally understood.

"He's gone," I said, trembling also and clasping my hands to hide it. "Back East."

"Too bad," he said. Then, "Come here."

This time I went, folded myself into his arms and cried. He rocked me in his arms, talking to me, telling me words like "it's not your fault," and kissing me until it was time for me to go.

❖   ❖   ❖

To most people our brief exchange would have been a mere puzzlement, with insufficient clues to draw meaning. But we were the wounded, the defiled, and the mutual encoding from our individual tragedies enabled us to communicate on a level which I had never before experienced.

In a strange sense, in the arms of this sixteen year old delinquent I found a sense of home. I have often wondered how my life would have turned out if someone else, a teacher, a neighbour, a doctor, or a pastor for instance, had been the first to give me that sense of being acknowledged and understood.

The strangest thing about that moment with Frank? Was that I felt forgiven, as if I had done something to be forgiven for. As if I had willingly withstood Richie's assaults, as if the bed-wetting, the constant headaches, the terror of night sweats, the anger that rose unsummoned at the most unexpected moments, were a result of my behavior and not Richie's.

As if the hypervigilant watch I kept on every man in my family's social circle was a paranoia I embraced. As if I were not the victim.

And it's funny how what happens to you affects how you feel about yourself. How something not of your own causation can feel like something you failed at, something you did wrong, something you are somehow guilty of.

I began to worry that even God would reject me, that maybe he had rejected me already during the first encounter with Richie. After all, Dr. Metralkis, the police appointed psychiatrist, had said as much.

"You seem very much alone in your life." She observed during a one hour session. "You have nothing in common with your parents and you say you have friends but oddly, you do not socialize much with them."

"I have God. Jesus. He is always with me."

"Oh really?" Carefully articulated brows rose, above penetrating eyes, as she leveled her gaze at me. "And where was he, this God, while an eleven year old child was repeatedly attacked, molested?"

She drew deeply on a cigarette, and carefully rolled the ash off into the crystal ashtray. The large rings she wore fascinated me, their stones set like chunks of faceted pale blue sky and winter suns glittering on short, stubby fingers.

She was a stout, expensively tailored woman, and I looked across at her, my slax and sweater set seeming too colorful, my blue bead necklace a plastic imitation of nothing precious. She took another draught of her cigarette, waiting for my response.

I folded my hands and said, "The Bible says we are not tried beyond what we are capable of enduring."

"Oh so God intended you to endure this horrible assault, did he?"

"I don't think so, but…"

"But you don't know, do you?"

"God loves me, I know that for sure."

"Did God come down out of the sky with a flaming sword and a big white horse to protect you?" She tilted her head and her gaze stuck me like a pin impaling an insect.

"No!" She answered her own question, her words emphatic, powerful as she stubbed out the cigarette, her jeweled fingers twisting, pressing the lengthy butt into the dirty ash.

"He left you, a small child, alone in the presence of this monster. A monster, by the way, which according to Christian belief, he also created. For God is the god of all creation, is he not?"

I was fifteen years old. All those years my hope was in Christ. No matter what had happened to me, how horrible and unthinkable and yes, unspeakable it was, God knew all, and still he loved me. God was the one being who heard all of my thoughts, and found them acceptable, who I could speak to again and again about any and every thing that troubled me.

God embraced me into his family, the only family wherein I had a sense of belonging. Believing this had sustained me for two years through a living hell and in the years afterward and in a just a very few moments in a starkly furnished office, Dr. Metralkis had all but stripped me of my one comfort, my one successful alliance—an alliance with the Almighty.

"We can't understand," I began, my hands twisting nervously in my lap, "We're only human…"

"If there is a God why didn't he rescue you?" she persisted.

The question burned in my consciousness day after day, year after year. But in that moment, the only words I could remember were the ones Christ spoke in agony on the cross. Silent and screaming, they echoed through me: *My God, my God, why hast thou forsaken me?*

CHAPTER 21

Saturday August 10ᵗʰ, 1963
Dear Diary,

Beach party day! and my life is perfect. After my chores, I'm going shopping just like Sandra Dee does in the movies. I'll buy myself any outfit I want, cause I got paid yesterday, and then Damion will pick me up, and we'll get Jillian and drive to Deep Cove. My life is like, utterly fab.

Margaret Jean.

The sun beat down on our little white house, a joyous thing for a picnic day, and yet, I awoke with butterflies in my tummy. Oh yes. Poor Nick. He would be festering all day. And rightfully so. It was mean to exclude him from the party when he could just as well have come. And I knew that feeling, that feeling of being left out.

❖　❖　❖

That feeling took me all the way back to the seventh grade. In those days, elementary school ended at grade six and you went up to junior high in seventh grade. There were no graduations: those were reserved for grade twelve students; people who had completed the first major phase of the educational journey.

Everyone was struggling to achieve some sort of status, to find their place in the sudden melee of young teens coming from all the outlying districts to one school. I hadn't been popular in elementary school, and I was hoping my anonymity in the new mix would change that in high school. It didn't.

My earliest memory of junior high is an HPD (Health and Personal Development) class. The teacher was late coming in (perhaps by agreement?) and Cindy Hall and Louise Carson were up at the blackboard writing names. Above the names was the date and place of a party. I can't recall either. But the name of every person in the room was on that board. Except mine.

Nobody looked at me. My friend, Jenina, wouldn't even talk to me. We had been friends from the age of three, when we were neighbours in Millstream and kept up an on and off again acquaintance all through elementary school. When we were very little, we'd wander through the woods together, play by the streams, argue and occasionally fight. Jenina never forgot that I pushed her into the creek once, and I couldn't for the life of me remember doing so.

And now in this classroom, far from the isolated hillocks and forests, I had no idea why my name wasn't on the list. I think that was the worst aspect of the situation, even more frustrating than the humiliation of being uninvited.

Maybe somehow, being the target of a pervert for the better part of two years had wiped out any social skills I might have accumulated in spite of my Asperger's.

Or maybe part of it was that having suffered a particularly nasty and unspeakable injustice that no one wanted to hear about had left me feeling isolated and defensive, but just how that social disconnection flowed over to a party invitation, I had no idea. I suppose it had nothing to do with my past and everything to do with my odd and unpredictable thirteen year old behaviour.

"They forgot my name." I told Jenina after class.

"They didn't forget," she said.

"Will you ask them if I can come?" I said.

"I can't do that," Jenina said.

"But you're invited."

"And you're not." Jenina hurried off down the hall, lest she be seen talking with me.

Jenina and I had been friends forever. As I watched her back disappear down the hall, my social inadequacy overwhelmed me. I had no clue why I wasn't invited. But I knew instinctively asking Cindy and Louise would just give them an opportunity to further humiliate me. After awhile I got used to not being invited. I found a different set to mingle with, different all the time.

❖　❖　❖

Yes, I knew how it felt to be left out. But I hadn't cried, not even then. Nick's tears left me cold. If he had turned to me and said, "Fine. Give me a call when you're done with this guy. If I'm still interested, maybe we'll talk." If he had said something like that, I could have respected him. But he didn't. He cried and said he needed to be with me and suddenly I was the strong person in the relationship. That terrified me.

As for Damion, I couldn't really pinpoint how I felt about him. As I stretched my arms above my head, I remembered how kissing him had started warm, tingling feelings. But when I imagined him cupping my breast in his hand like Nick sometimes did, I knew I would never let that happen with Damion.

Why? As I slid out of bed and slipped on a pair of shorts, I realized there was some softness about Damion, a kind of ripeness of flesh that came with age, and after Richie, older men were repulsive to me. Damion wasn't fat or overweight, but Nick had that firmness that follows the last growth spurt; lean muscle and firm buttocks.

Softness in men turned me off. I needed protection from predatory old men, men who'd lived hard lives in the military or on the farm. I needed a man who knew how to get dirty, do hard work, fight with his fists and think with his brain.

And now, look at Nick, crying like a baby. What good did it do to be lean and sharp if you were just a big crybaby? I had never cried over a lost love. Ever. Dr. Metralkis, my police-appointed psychiatrist, put it succinctly. "You have the rare capacity, my dear, to turn love on and off. Just like water in a faucet." She nodded, leaning back in her armchair and eyeing me through her cigarette smoke. She made a twisting motion with her wrist and hand. "Like turning off a tap."

❖   ❖   ❖

CHAPTER 22

It was the Spring of 1962 and I was still fifteen years old when the police finally found me. I'd run away from home, taken refuge with some young married kids from Al-Anon.

I just couldn't take being home anymore, everything felt mixed up and crazy and I'd never been able to tell my parents about Richie. I was on nerve tonics, and the headaches wouldn't quit. I was so addicted to Aspirins that I'd buy the little tins of them and take all the pills at once.

My homework wasn't getting done. I was having a lot of trouble in school, skipping classes and not being able to keep up in Science or Socials and frankly, there was no-one in my family I felt I could turn to. So I just asked Anna and Joe if I could stay with them for a couple of weeks while I thought things through, and they said sure.

The apartment was located in James Bay, at that time an area of rather run down properties near the water. I wasn't going to school, and I didn't have a job, so I had plenty of time to review my present situation.

And looking back I deeply regretted letting Daniel Cormier go. We'd gone steady from September to December in the year I turned fifteen. And my sudden longing for him sucked the marrow from my bones and left me weak and strangely angry. Angry with myself for refusing to go with him when he left to find work in Ontario. Why had I refused him? I could not recall, could only see his dark curly mess of hair, large capable hands, and laughing blue eyes. Why then, had I refused him?

Ah yes. The blue mohair sweater. See, Richie had brought me a chocolate bar that first time he abused me. And now, I couldn't sort out the gift thing. I was stuck on the fact that surprise gifts only came from bad men. People who wanted to hurt me.

Now, if I was *with* a boy when he bought me a gift, I was fine. I knew the source, and I presumed to know what came with the gift, which was simply friendship. But a gift sprung on me? That was a huge unknown, a threat that I felt at the deepest level.

Intellectually, I knew I was wrong, but I just couldn't suppress the deep-seated fear and misgiving I felt when a boy I was romantically involved with gave me a gift. And Daniel had given me a beautiful blue mohair sweater for Christmas. Lord knows how long he saved up to buy it. They were the 'in' thing that year, all the girls had them, and of course I didn't. It was a very sweet thing to do. And the very reason I broke up with him immediately after.

Anyway, he'd gone out to Ontario alone, and here I was, bunking in with a couple just starting out in life with hardly enough furniture and room for themselves, let alone me. I just didn't know what to do or where to go. I had no money and no job and no prospects. I was halfway through grade ten and I had nothing going for me. When the police showed up with my mother, I felt a tinge of relief. If ever I was prepared to embrace my mother, to be open and clear with her, to have a true and cleansing heart to heart that would bond us forever, this was the moment.

"You'd best be going home, now," the officer said.

"Mom," I said, "it's just, you have no idea what happened to me."

"With Richie, you mean?" she said. I was surprised. And confused. She looked at me, then away, kind of embarrassed. "I'm not stupid!" she said.

What on earth did that mean? My mind reeled, while I struggled to understand what she meant by that. The cop stared down at the toes of his boots, his face red. My mother pursed her lips and set her jaw, still avoiding my eyes.

Everything I had ever hoped for from my family vanished in that moment. Every connection with parents, family, and community dissolved in those words. It was incomprehensible to me that my mother could have known and not stepped up to protect me. And instead of anger, I felt a terrible, soul-wrenching disappointment, a decaying of something integral inside me, a fomenting bitterness and a deep, unrelenting sadness. If my own mother wouldn't fight for me, wouldn't care for me, no-one would. Only the Eddy C.s and the Frank de Courcys of the world, defiant soldiers fighting bravely in their own unacknowledged battles, would ever fight for me. That I knew for certain.

And in that moment I made up my mind. I would go home. I would mind my P's and Q's as we used to say, doing my chores, minding my parents, and I would get a free education and room and board, which I had come to learn were precious commodities. But I would never be their daughter. I would never belong. Obviously, that was already the case and always had been.

I suppose this was unfair to my father, who, as far as I knew, was never told. If he was, he never saw fit to mention it to me. Richie was long gone by then, having packed up his family and moved back to Winnipeg, and I suppose my mother thought there was no point making a fuss about it. Perhaps she had only figured things out afterward, or maybe in her reluctance to discuss all things sexual, she simply found herself unable to broach the subject.

I do not know, and we never developed the kind of relationship that could approach such a matter.

And in this sense of isolation I needed someone set like a rock, someone tough enough to look out for me, tender enough to love me and man enough to keep me safe. Not a cry baby. Not someone who broke down over a silly thing like a date. I had wanted to love Nick forever, to be his wife, to live out our lives in that solemn and sweet relationship we had cultivated. And now I could not. I simply positively and absolutely could not.

❖ ❖ ❖

"What happens that you 'break up' with these boys—when you end the relationship?" Metralkis had asked in one of our sessions.

I shrugged. "I just get the feeling that it's time to move on," I said candidly.

"But you feel a strong attachment for them before that?"

"Oh yes," I agreed. "Definitely strong feelings."

"And then--?"

"It's best to move on. You know, before things get…serious."

"And so what happens to these feelings you talk about?"

"They stop."

"Just like that?" Smoke curled up around her shoulders and snaked off into the shadows beyond.

I nodded. "Just like that."

"This is not possible."

I sighed. "Yes, Doctor, it is possible. I do it all the time."

❖　❖　❖

It wasn't that I wanted someone like Frank to come back and fix things for me. Or even Daniel Cormier. Intellectually I knew Nick was a good man and a solid catch. But I couldn't for the life of me get over the feeling of nothingness now associated with him. I wanted to love him, but I couldn't. I could not forgive him his tears. I could not make myself so vulnerable.

CHAPTER 23

After Richie, I couldn't trust women, because none of the women I had trusted to care for and protect me would believe me, would even explore what I was saying or give it any credence.

The people I had trusted, men and women alike, had let me down. I guess I felt it was only natural for men—they were after something. But at some unconscious level the women in my life comprised a key part of my culture and to be denied their belief constituted not only betrayal but excommunication. I was a child with nowhere to turn, no-one to value and nurture me, alone in a circle of women, unacknowledged and unworthy. In denying me, they disenfranchised me, exorcising me from their feminine community.

And from all these experiences, from my aunts and friend not believing about Richie, from my mother saying she knew, from the school girls leaving me out of their party invitation, I came to one incontrovertible conclusion: I did not understand women.

Ironically, some of the most popular girls were the ones who shoplifted, lied, cheated, back-talked the teachers and then bragged about it. Not only that, they were mean. They had lying and bullying down to a fine art. Asperger me, I simply could not understand what made them so popular, and I foolishly said so.

I couldn't just go along with that kind of behaviour. I remember once hearing about some girls ripping all the plants out of some old lady's garden just because she had publicly chastised them. Being fully aware of how labour-intensive flower beds could be, and of my grandmother's pride in hers, I could not even conceive of such an act.

One popular girl was worthy of admiration in my estimation; Gemma Hadley. I never heard her say a mean word about anyone, and she threw a year end party at her home on the lake every year, to which the entire class was invited. But Gemma seemed to be one of a few rare exceptions, and I was never in a position to be what you could call "friends" with her.

As a result, the entire female species was as foreign to me as a Zebra to a long-horned steer. I had no idea whatsoever how to get in with the girls, how those social networks happened and were maintained.

But I knew what men were about. I could, to some degree at least, be popular with them. I could be sexually attractive without having sexual intercourse. It honestly never occurred to me that I could *not* have one without the other. And in fact, I was successful.

In spite of being sexually molested for two years by Richie, I was technically a virgin until my engagement to Karl Stein in the spring of 1964, and so from grades eight through twelve, I was known as a tease. Not only that, but my walk, my smile, was so promiscuous that people just assumed I had sex with the boys who took me out.

Part of this exaggerated behavior was of course, due to the Asperger's. Unable to interpret social cues or learn social behavior from observing others, but very adept at book learning, I took everything I knew about attracting men from Movie magazines.

The larger than life images of sexy stars like Kim Novak, Elizabeth Taylor, and my favorite, Sophia Loren, were engraved on my consciousness. I saw how they walked, how they smiled, how they lured men—all on the big screen or in magazines.

None of it was real, but it was up front and visual and I could learn from that. It was obvious behavior that I could easily copy, and in my Asperger's way, I did, without understanding that it was, even for the actresses, artificial.

The result was extreme and undoubtedly alarming behavior –every smile was a flirtation. Boys and men really liked it, and they all assumed they knew where it would lead. Some who knew me least well even bragged that they had made it "all the way".

Take for instance a time when I was fifteen, and my boyfriend was Daniel Cormier. In spite of being Catholic, he hung out with the Molsen boys, who were staunch Baptists and just happened to attend my church. Now, my parents were extremely strict. I was not allowed to go to any of the school dances or parties, or the community dances.

This was partly because of a news item about the community dances. It was only natural these events would make the news—they were always the talk of the school the Monday after a weekend dance. These events were held out in Sooke and were famous for knife and fist fights.

The news story centered around a girl commonly known as Bloody Mary. It seems she had an unfaithful boyfriend, and at one dance, after getting good and drunk, she took off after him with a knife.

Such excitement and carryings on! My parents didn't want me anywhere near that sort of thing. The world was going to hell on a racetrack what with Elvis Presley gyrating all over the stage and singing that "devil-inspired" music.

So I was only allowed to go to church events, like "Young People's Meetings", a dry, Bible study gathering that happened in the little brown Baptist church once a week. The kind of meetings where the mild and stubborn, frog-shaped Pastor Moorhouse condemned dancing and drinking, much to every teen's dismay.

The Molsens went, and Daniel came with them. Daniel, a Catholic, came to be with me, which meant as long as I was going out with Daniel, the Molsens also picked me up. We would drive to where Daniel left his car parked, and Daniel and I would progress from there. I was not allowed to date boys in their cars until I was sixteen, but going to Young People's with the Molsens did not constitute a date, and so it passed my parent's scrutiny. That one hour at the meetings (we did attend), and the half hour or so we stole together afterwards, talking and sharing a coke, constituted our relationship—along with time on the phone, of course.

Although we were "going steady" which meant we did not date anyone else, Daniel, at seventeen, liked to party, albeit without me. One Saturday night, about ten o'clock, I got a phone call.

"Margaret?"

"Daniel, darling." (I was *so* Elizabeth Taylor).

"Do you know anyone named Pete Moss?"

"Peatmoss?" I laughed. "You're joking, right."

"No," he said somewhat impatiently, "I'm not."

"Well, isn't that the stuff you put on your garden?" I giggled.

"Will you be serious for a minute, Margaret?" Daniel was angry. I stopped giggling.

"What's going on, Danny, where are you?"

"I'm at a party in Metchosin and there's some guy here, his name is Pete Moss and he says he knows you. Says he took you out."

"What? Pete Moss? He's crazy. I don't know anybody by that name. I've *never* known anybody by that name." I paused for a millisecond to think and added, "The only Peter I know is Peter Patterson, and I've never been out with him, either. Are you sure Pete Moss is his real name? It sounds phony to me."

"You've never been out with the guy."

"Never."

"You're sure."

"Daniel, I've never even *met* him!"

At young people's the following Tuesday, David Molsen took me aside. "So you heard what happened last weekend?" he asked, grinning.

I wondered why he was asking. "Sure. Danny went to a party. So what?" I didn't expect him to live in a cloister, just because I was imprisoned in my home. Well, that's what it felt like at fifteen.

"He didn't tell you, then?"

"Tell me what?"

"You really don't know?"

"I have no idea what you're talking about."

David's grin broke into laughter. "Some guy at the party was bad-mouthing you."

"Bad-mouthing me?" Why was that funny, I wondered.

"He said he'd been out with you and you went all the way with him on the first date."

I blushed crimson. I was furious. I was about to protest that I'd never even met the creep when David laughed again. He knew me too well from driving Daniel and I around, to believe the story either.

"Don't worry. Danny took care of him. He phoned you, right?"

I nodded.

"Soon's he hung up, he walks over to this Pete guy, taps him on the shoulder, asks him outside.

They get out there, the guy puts his dukes up and Danny decks him. Pow! Right in the jaw. Laid him out flat. 'That's for Margaret Adam' he says. This Pete guy? his friends took him to the hospital. Now he's all wired up."

"Wired up?"

"Yeah. Dan broke his jaw."

Pete Moss wasn't the only one. A lot of boys claimed the privilege. The girls believed it because apparently (and I have no memory of this) I told my grade eight HPD class that I wasn't a virgin. Imagine that! I can't, frankly. Aside from not remembering ever having made the statement, I can only think that I was trying indirectly to raise the issue of my abuse within an institutional setting, testing the waters to see if there was any support to be had from that arena.

Perhaps I did not specifically say I was not a virgin, but something else that made Leslie think I wasn't, and it impressed itself in that way in her mind. Others who were in the same class don't recall the statement.

But forty years later, over lunch, Leslie laughed and said, "We knew you'd been around then, see." Even then, in the pub, with three of our other old classmates, I didn't correct her, didn't explain.

There is no appropriate place for conversations about sexual abuse.

So, one way or another, whether it was what I said, or what my looks and manner implied, or all of the above, a lot of my contemporaries assumed I was having sex with every boy I ever dated (and there were plenty), and so they just verbally leapt on the band wagon.

The truth was, the reason I didn't often go steady, was because, after my experience with Richie, I didn't want to have sex. And I couldn't help but notice that after dating for any length of time, having sex (judging from the overtures I dealt with) seemed to be a natural progression in the dating scheme.

I also heard stories in the washrooms about couples who were dating for several weeks or months having sex, and so I knew it wasn't just my reputation that encouraged these overtures.

So, to be safe, I usually just dated for awhile, a few weeks at most, and then broke it off. In fact, I dated so many different boys that if my mother answered the phone and a boy asked for me, she would tell them frankly to stay away from me because I'd break their heart. Naturally, this only fanned the flames.

Nick and Daniel Cormier were the only exceptions to my short life-span dating rule. They had respect. They understood how I felt, and they honored that. Strangely enough, Frank de Courcy did too. Perhaps that's why these men hold a special place in my heart even today.

There was some hot and heavy petting in the back seats of cars, but my introduction to womanhood took place on a moonlit beach with my very capable fiancée, Karl Stein when I was seventeen. (I was always falling in love. It was my *escape*.) And if, after all the talk he'd heard about me, he was surprised to find me a virgin, he never said so.

CHAPTER 24

Exotic. Looking back, that's how I'd describe him, with his olive skin and dark eyes, green around the iris, a fleck of yellow just above the lower lid. Karl Stein and I had been acquaintances in school, me two grades below him. He'd see me walking into the gym and motion for me to sit with him at basketball games, or if we happened to meet in the hallway between classes, he'd always say "Hi, Li'l Sis!" Karl was an only child, and so he had "adopted' me as his sister. He'd open the door for me as we walked, chatting, down the hallways. Sometimes we'd sit together at lunch time, or kill time in conversation after school. We never socialized on weekends; actually never off the school grounds.

Karl joined the Air Force right out of high school. In those days, the forces were separate and highly competitive units. When Karl came back on leave, he stopped to visit his old high school. I just happened to be walking down the hallway on my way out, when the doors flung open and in strode Karl, resplendent in his blue-grey air force uniform. His eyes lit up. "Little Sis!" We rushed toward each other and he swooped me up in his arms. He held me for a while and then kissed me. After that kiss we both knew I couldn't be his "little sister' any more.

We talked, walking down the hall together, his arm around me, his hand in mine. We were suddenly reluctant to let each other go. I did have to get home, however. He asked if he could call me. I gave him my number and headed home.

As our relationship developed, I learned that Karl was adopted. I also learned that his easy-going nature did not come from his adoptive mother, a bridge club woman whose husband was a pharmacist. She had plans for her adopted son, and only child: Karl was going places and he needed the right wife to get him there. With Mrs. Stein impelling them along, of course. Karl had a history with a private school girl, named Stephanie, one of those upper class girls with perfect manicures and clothes that constituted a fall and summer wardrobe. Someone who, along with her parents, was appropriately educated and socialized. The fact that Stephanie had gotten pregnant by Karl out of wedlock, and had to give the baby up for adoption, didn't seem to matter a whit to Mrs. Stein, who spared no opportunity to make me aware of my lack in all the above categories.

Maybe if the television shows of the day had been different, I might have had a chance. In my day, it was Father Knows Best, Leave it to Beaver, Walt Disney (I saw myself as Annette) and Dr. Welby. The programs taught us to be nice, to get along, to trust in your own integrity and eventually everyone else will come around. Be good, be nice, be polite, behave. There was no "Friends", no acerbic commentary between people who had intimate knowledge of each other. The only manipulators were Lucy and Ethel, and it was all in good fun. Or maybe that's just my personal cop out. I know my sister, Terry, when she grew up would have been more than capable of dealing with Mrs. Stein. I was not.

I had bought some pink fabric and Mrs. Stein was an expert seamstress. She suggested we make a dress together. I remember my hands sweating and trembling when I sewed with her. Sewing was a novel experience for me. The girls that came from Saskatchewan to help out did the sewing in our house--them or Mom. Not me. I had failed Home Economics miserably. The teacher gave me a passing grade, saying: "Promise you'll take art?"

I remember nodding frantically "Yes! I promise!"

And the teacher responding, "You'll never sew anything anyway, and I won't have to waste my time ripping out your seams."

Working on this project with Mrs. S. made me wish I'd paid attention at some time, any time, in that class. I didn't have to worry. Mrs. S. took complete control of the project, and when she learned that I no idea what "the grain" was, she very capably proceeded to whip up the simple shift. When the dress was finished, and pressed, she held it out to me and said, "Here. Put it on, dear, let's have a look."

I went in to a room and put it on. It was very warm in their house, and I was very nervous. I wanted to rinse off my underarms and pat them dry, but Mrs. Stein waited between me and the bathroom. I dabbed my underarms with my slip and discovered nylon's lack of absorbency. Oh well, nothing to do but try on the dress. It was a shift, shaped by a few darts, zipperless, with a wide neck. I slid it on over my head, adjusted the waist, slipped on my shoes and went out into the living room.

Mrs. Stein looked me up and down. "Sephanie would have been drop dead gorgeous in that dress."

Nevertheless, Karl and I got engaged. I had my misgivings, but accepted his engagement ring.

I showed it to Mom and Maria, who would later remind me of the mistake I made, letting Karl go.

"Your mother hates me," I told Karl.

"I'll ask to be assigned to Newfoundland," Karl told me. "It's beautiful there, lots of ocean, lots of sky. And there's a great theatre group. We'll have a dozen kids and you'll march them all off to rehearsals. We'll have a fabulous life." I drew a deep breath. Maybe. Maybe. Lord knew I wanted to get away from my family.

One afternoon when Mrs. Stein was telling me that Karl was her whole life, I ventured to say that when Karl was away, she must miss him terribly.

"Oh, it's just training. He's not gone long."

"But if he's stationed somewhere far away?"

"My dear, when Karl gets married, I'm not losing a son. I'm gaining a daughter. When Karl is permanently stationed, we'll move."

That ended that.

In retrospect, I had a couple of opportunities to marry fine young men. Good men. I threw them all away. Somewhere deep inside, I felt I wasn't worthy and their mothers picked up on that. They declared war right at the starting gate and I wasn't up for it.

❖   ❖   ❖

CHAPTER 25

The truth was, I had battle fatigue. At least, that's what it felt like. I couldn't even sleep in peace. Not at night anyway. I'd wake, rising up out of bed like a person drowning, clawing my way to awakeness, to a place where I was still all in one piece. I would sit upright, breathing hard, sweat streaming from my brow, a bloody sweat trickling down my chest, a cold dampness at the nape of my neck.

For several moments I'd remain motionless, pinioned by horror. When I had finally steeled myself, I'd leap out of bed, landing as far from the bed and as close to the lightswitch at the door as possible. A second leap and I was at the light switch flicking it on.

Even with the light on, I had to force myself to bend down and look under the bed. *Oh God thank you thank you thank you that it's not real.* Sixteen years old and still looking under that damn bed, just the same as when I was eleven. How could you tell anybody that? You couldn't. It was impossible to explain.

The nightmare is repetitive. It is always the same. There is never any deviation. In the dream I am in a cauldron. I am being boiled alive. The pot is one of those black cast iron round jobs that cowboy cooks hang over the fire. Only it's huge, bigger than any of those and I am in it and up to my chest in steaming water.

There is no burning sensation, and that is somehow the most terrifying thing of all. The woman cooking me is dressed in black clothes that swath and hide her. I cannot see her face, only her hands on the huge stick she uses to stir the broth around me.

The woman, the witch, for I know that's what she is, takes my hand and puts it to her lips and begins to nibble on my finger tips. I draw back in horror, try to pull away but my fingertips fall off in her mouth. I cannot believe this is happening to me! Joint by joint bits of my fingers pull off easily, and I come to the ridiculous conclusion it is because I am well done. I am like an overcooked chicken, easily pulled apart at the joints.

She reaches for more of me, pulls off another bit of finger, this time my ring finger, and I am whining, begging, pleading with her "Don't hurt me, please don't hurt me, please!"

And even as I say this, I realize she isn't *hurting* me. There is no pain. And then logic takes me to the rationale that if there is no pain, I must be dead. I died and I'm in hell. And I surge awake, sweat-soaked and panicking, too terrified to cry out, too ashamed to run to my parents for help. I am sixteen. It is only a dream.

Some nights when the moon is full, I don't bother with the light. It is a test of courage, remaining in the silvered dark. The real bravery is in getting out of bed, putting my feet on the floor, there, just there at the edge of the bed.

For in my dreams she haunts the depths of blackness beneath the bed. She waits for me to slip, to fall, to drown in sleep so she can gorge on me. And I know it's nonsense, so I make myself put my feet down, steadily, firmly. First one foot and then, when the first is unaccosted, the other. And I find my slacks in the moonlight and slip them on, and I find a sweater and pull it over my head, and I slip canvas shoes on my feet. Then I stand perfectly still and listen.

If there is only silence, no creaking of stairways or floorboards, no flushing of toilets or closing of bathroom doors, only silence and darkness, then I go to my window and lift it out of its frame and set it down beside the dresser. It is a big window, about five feet high and three feet wide. It is my gateway to peace and freedom and safety. Because one thing I know for sure, there is no safety in any building where men breathe and live and sleep. The only safe place is out there in God's creation.

I lift my leg over the sill and the lilac bush weaves and rustles, wafting its perfume at me, and I see the fir trees moving in the wind and that is so perfect, for the wind is like the breath of God. It soothes me.

In the moonlit yard, I find the path through the back acreage to the Crossley's house behind us and Meaford Road beyond that, and turn left down the hill to where the road dead ends. And there I enter a narrow fringe of woods, and brushing aside Oregon Grape and Juniper berry bushes dwarfed by tall firs, I press through the shadows to what I know lies beyond—Colwood Golf Course.

The moonlit beauty of the manicured lawns and the towering trees takes my breath away. An owl calls, and in the distance a dog barks. Directly ahead, about a hundred yards away stands a huge tree. Joy fills my heart as I walk to the towering grey trunk, the branches high above me wind-tossed. Overhead stars blaze like loose diamonds spilled onto black velvet. I settle my back against the massive trunk, feeling peaceful, safe. Finally I can breathe easy. I can rest.

Is it my Asperger's that makes me feel as if I belong with the living, stolid tree more than with my busy parents? I cannot put into words this sense of companionship. Cannot explain the security the rough-textured massiveness of the trunk gives me. It is too complicated to try. I just want to close my eyes and sleep, but I dare not.

To not be home, for anyone to go into my room and find my window out and me gone would mean the end of this pleasant escape. Dad for sure would nail the window shut and I would be trapped in that house, in that room with my nightmares forever.

So I rest awhile, breathe the fresh-dew smell of the night, trace the rough edge of the grey tree bark, sit and stare dreamy-eyed at the stars until something in me says that it is time to go.

Even then, I could not say how that happened. How I knew when it was time to go. A sudden compelling urge to leave now. At once. To hurry back to the path through the woods, my footsteps now urgent, fear of being caught suddenly sweeping over me, and I run through the woods, up the road, past the Crossley house, past the tire swing and the chicken coop and the woodshed and slip over the sill into my room.

I hear footsteps in the kitchen. I whip off my sweater and slacks, my pant leg stuck on my shoe.

I hear the kettle filling with water, the sound of a spoon against a cup, and I give one fierce tug and the pant leg comes off, the shoe with it, and I throw them into a corner as I hear footsteps descending the two steps down to the hall by my bedroom. Grams is at the door.

"Having trouble sleeping dear?" she asks, without turning on the light.

"I'm okay. How about you, Grams?" I have the covers pulled up under my chin, hoping she doesn't spot my PJ's on the floor.

"Indigestion. Probably the gravy."

I nod in the darkness.

"Is your window open, dear?" she asks as the curtain billows in the wind.

"I woke up sweating," I said.

"Tsk, Tsk. Well, you'd better get to sleep now. It's after three."

CHAPTER 26

Later Saturday, Beach Party Day;
Dear Diary,

I love my new outfit. I bought the coolest white pedal pushers and a pink and white striped blouse with a Sandra Dee collar. Saw Clark downtown; he offered me a ride home, but he and a bunch of kids were going somewhere else first and I just wanted to get home, and soak in the tub.

❖ ❖ ❖

Mom and I hardly ever did anything together, except housework. You know, like canning red beets and cleaning out the boys' rooms. But one thing we did do was shopping at Eddy's on Douglas Street in Victoria every fall before school started. Or just after.

Mom had a charge account there in the days before credit cards were invented. We'd head out in the old Austin Morris, and I had a limit: two skirts, two blouses or sweater sets and no slacks.

Slacks had to come out of my babysitting money because in those days girls were not allowed to wear slacks to school. Unless it was snowing. Then we were allowed to wear our slacks under our skirts, but as soon we got into the school, we would crowd into the washrooms to take off our slacks and pack them away. Slacks were strictly forbidden. And jeans in those days were only for leisure or work wear.

Mom was on a really tight budget. She worked in the Empress Laundry or maybe it was at the Glenshields Motel cleaning rooms by then. The steam in the laundry got to her lungs.

But I remember this one year I was fifteen years old and she let me buy two mohair skirts, one blue plaid. I don't remember what colour the other one was because blue is my favourite color. And I got a blue lamb's wool sweater set, a pullover and cardigan, to match.

"You need a coat," Mom said.

Only because my friend, Clark, from college had recently bought me a gorgeous red coat. Yes, Clark was in college, and I was only in high school. But we had been friends like forever. He outlasted all my boyfriends and hoped one day to finally achieve romantic recognition. But with Clark, the chemistry just wasn't there. He was a terrific guy, though.

He lived in Oak Bay—an old money district, where I had a friend named Cheryl from the Maple Bay Bible Camp, Camp Imadene. Anyway, Clark and I spotted the coat downtown at The Bay, at the time, The Hudson's Bay Company. I don't remember what we were doing in town, but I remember that coat.

It was an A-line cut in a fabulous new fabric that felt like colored, textured foam. It was warm, lightweight, and looked like something Audrey Hepburn might wear in *Breakfast At Tiffany's*. It looked terrific on me, and so Clark bought it because he really really wanted to and I didn't have a coat and when I protested he said *it's only fifteen dollars*.

When I got home and showed Mom and Dad the coat, Dad's face got red and Mom called me a slut. And so two months later at Eddy's she was trying to get me a 'decent' coat. A dark teal wool job. It was Okay. I took it.

That coat cost her a lot. But it was worth it to her, I guess. Maybe she felt they had failed me by not making sure I had a coat. Or maybe she just wanted me to look invisible like her.

❖　❖　❖

The truth is I was pretty much finished with Nick after the crying episode. And, I reminded myself, if I was going to make a career of this acting business, then I had to get my priorities straight. After all, this was a once in a lifetime chance. A bit of Shakespeare came to mind, a play we'd taken in Miss Charles's English class. Julius Ceasar:

There is a tide in the affairs of men,
Which, taken at the flood, leads on to fortune;
Omitted, all the voyage of their life
Is bound in shallows and in miseries.
    Julius Ceasar, Act IV Sc. 3.

Look at Mom! And I could almost feel my life slipping downhill into the same drudgery; vacuuming, washing floors, putting up preserves. I could be at just such a turning point, right now, right this very instant and if I didn't go for it, I could drift right back into my old horrible life. I'd end up married, with babies and diapers and sinks full of dirty dishes. Working in a menial job and doing laundry over a wringer washer on my days off. Sorry, Nick! I mouthed, as I pushed my hair into wavy curls and went out into the hallway.

CHAPTER 27

When I came into the kitchen dressed and ready for breakfast, Mom and Dad were talking at the chrome and arborite table. Grams came in just then, through the back door, wearing her wide-brimmed straw hat, an apron and housedress. She had some medical looking tools in a bowl; tweezers, a small scalpel. She looked tired but triumphant.

"Those swallows in the barn all have worms!" she announced. I shuddered.

"It took me awhile but I think I got them all." Grams was a nurse and never quite got it out of her system. Once, much to her delight, I got impetigo on my knees. She'd heat this nasty grey paste called Thermafuge to the boiling point, slather it on a bunch of gauzy cloths and slap it directly on my open and bleeding knee, pretty much sending me right through the roof. Naturally, I was admonished to not cry or scream. I screamed my brains out. In my estimation, Grams and Mrs. W. were cut from the same cloth.

"Don't know why you bother to keep those birds alive." Dad complained. "They make such a mess."

"They're all God's creatures." Grams replied, untying her hat and setting it on the table. She took her bowl of instruments to the sink.

"Now what are you going to do with those, Mother?" Dad asked. His cautionary tone was not missed by any of us. Except Grams, who ignored it. The only person in our entire household who dared do such a thing.

"Well, the instruments have to be cleaned." She said, stopping the sink, turning the hot water on full blast and squeezing dish soap into the mix. As she plunged the tools into the midst, I looked at Dad. I thought he was going to faint. All the blood drained from his face and he winced.

"Geez!" Dad said, turning away. He was very sensitive about what went into the kitchen sink.

"I'll have to boil them afterward," Grams continued as if she hadn't heard him. Sometimes that's the best way with Dad, if you can get away with it.

I glanced over at Mom. She didn't look happy. What's new. But this morning she had a stubborn set to her jaw.

"Well?" she said to Dad, continuing a conversation that had been interrupted.

"Now, look here." Dad began, which told me it was all over already. *Now look here* means Dad's mind is made up and nothing short of a head transplant is going to change it. "I promised Jimmy I'd bring my bench saw out for a job he's got to do, and I intend to keep my word."

Jimmy was Kitty's second husband, which I thought maybe accounted for the fact that they had half a dozen or so kids with different last names, something almost unheard of in the '60's.

Kitty had bright mischievous eyes, and wonderfully freckled bosoms that peeked out from the low-necked, pretty, housedresses she sewed. Kitty had a terrific sense of humour and great legs that took full advantage of the dance floor. When the music called for some good old fashioned doh-si-doh-ing, her full skirts would flare up to reveal layers of crinoline and those great legs and Dad would positively light up.

"Well, Jimmy said he's going to be in town this morning, and he'd be happy to pick up the saw." Mom should have known this was a lost cause because Dad never let anyone take his tools out of his sight. Not even my older brother Rob was allowed to use Dad's tools.

In fact, one time, Rob was somehow, in a brotherly way, mean to Scotty who spent a lot of time thinking up a way to get even. One day, he thought of just the thing. When Rob was at school and Dad was in town, Scotty snuck into Dad's tool box and took out a hammer and a chisel and a screw driver. Just a few odds and ends. Dug a hole in the back yard and buried them.

It was some weeks later, and Rob and Scotty had made everything up, when Dad went to use his hammer and found it gone. Well, sir, he didn't even stop to think. He just went straight for Rob.

Naturally, Rob denied using the hammer or any other tool. This just made Dad madder. "You keep lying to me and you're really going to get it!" Nonetheless, Rob kept protesting his innocence. Dad couldn't think of what else could have happened to his tools, so he took Rob out to the shed, handed him a pair of boxing gloves and then put on his own. In the army, in the 40's, Dad had been a golden gloves champion. Rob at fifteen, had no such training. It didn't matter, though. Dad took him for a round or two, getting in a few good punches, all the time telling Rob to "get his hands up" to protect his face. But then of course, Dad would just go for the ribs or the chest. Rob was angry as all get out for being accused of and then punished for something he didn't do, so the match was maybe a little better than Dad might have expected.

Scotty thought it was pretty funny. Not that he's a sadist or anything. But he was considerably younger and had already survived a strapping for helping Grams weed her garden. Only Grams wasn't there to point out the weeds and Scotty at five was not so botanically inclined. What he uprooted were mostly seedlings of lettuce, beets and corn. But then, when you're a little kid and just trying to be helpful, every little green growing thing looks pretty much alike.

I used to cry when Scotty got the strap. He was so little and it seemed so disproportionate to punish a small boy in that way. But Mom just shrugged when I tried to talk to her about it.

"Your grandfather used to take the horse whip to your dad," she said grimly, "so I think your Dad is doing pretty good."

Anyway, here was Mom, foolishly suggesting that Dad actually let his tools out of his sight, and not even to a member of the family. That suggestion was going nowhere.

"I don't lend out my tools unless I'm going to be around." Dad reiterated.

"But if you would, Jimmy could pick up the saw, we could both go to Charlie's funeral."

At this point, Grams added her two bits: "After all, Tommy," she said, "Charlie served in the war, same as you."

CHAPTER 28

Charlie and Cora were good friends to Mom and Dad, starting way back in the old days when we lived up on Millstream. My older brother and I used to love to see the jovial grey-haired man we called "Uncle Charlie" coming up the walk.

"Can you count to twenty?" Charlie'd ask me, and we knew he had Life Savers Candies, butterscotch for me, cherry for Rob. These were our reward for showing our cleverness. My brother would quickly recite the numbers to one hundred (he was older, so more was required of him), but I took longer; I had to get over the loathsome thirteen-fourteen combination to get to twenty.

I suppose it was some aspect of Asperger's, but for some reason, I hated the "r" syllables in those numbers, just dreaded saying them out loud. I'd always resort to a froggy croak when I came to those digits to protect myself from the sound.

This made Charlie throw back his head and laugh, but nonetheless, he gave me the candies I was so fond of before he and Cora and Mom and Dad all headed out for the evening.

One time, Dad went visiting in Saskatchewan and Mom and her sister, Aunt Rose, decided Mom should surprise Dad and get her driver's license.

Now, ever since she was twelve, Mom had driven any number of vehicles. Mostly in Saskatchewan. But the requirement for licensing came about, and Mom had been driving illegally in BC. Apparently this caused my father some concern, so the women thought legal driving status for Mom would be a nice surprise for Dad. They asked Charlie if he would help Edna. He gladly agreed, coming almost daily to take Mom for her "lesson". He even drove her down to take the test.

When Dad came back, after he unpacked and gave them the news from back home, the women folk gathered in the kitchen. When Dad came in to refill his coffee cup, Grams, Mom and her sister, Rose, proudly presented him with Mom's BC driver's license.

Dad stood holding his coffee cup. He had a tremor, and when he got upset his hand would visibly shake. Now the teacup began a jittery clicking against the saucer.

"Well?" Mom said, the only one who dared to break the now very tense silence. Dad set the cup down on the counter, a redness starting at his collar and moving slowly up his neck.

"Well, how about that?" Dad said, his eyes narrowing and his voice growing quiet. Rose relaxed, turned to get another cigarette out of her packet. Then Dad added, "The minute I'm out of town, you're off with Charlie!"

Somehow he made a vast leap to the conclusion that a great deal more than just driving lessons had been going on.

Anyone who knew Mom could only be shocked and disappointed at the very suggestion, but Dad stuck to his guns and banned Cora and Charlie, these great friends, from our home. Nothing the women said could change his mind.

"Well, I never!" Grams said, and steamed off into her room. Mom cried. Rose shook her head, held a match to her cigarette, inhaled and said, "Well, Tommy. I just don't know about you."

❖   ❖   ❖

And now that Charlie was dead, Mom wanted to show her respect for the couple who had only ever been good friends to them, and who had suffered a terrible injustice. But Dad was unmoved. To his dying day, he would believe Mom and Charlie had "something going on". Besides, Kitty and her amazing freckles now beckoned.

Dad stubbornly stuck to his stated position: "I didn't even know him during the war."

"It would be nice for Cora." Mom kneaded her left hand with her right.

"Well, you can go if you like. I've got a promise to keep." Dad stood up and pushed his chair in. Mom looked unsure if she had won or lost. She sighed. The promise Dad meant to keep probably had a lot more to do with Kitty than Jimmy. I looked at Mom. Personally, I would never have left my man alone with Kitty while Jimmy was busy out at the workbench with a saw, but as Mom stood up, she said, "Well, I guess I'll go by myself then." An unusual expression of independence for her.

❖   ❖   ❖

I bought a new pair of pedal pushers, a blouse with three-quarter sleeves and a stand-up, lapelled collar, and a white bathing suit. When Clark saw the bathing suit later that summer, he grinned.

"You know it's identical to the one Elizabeth Taylor wore in that movie, you know that, don't you?" he said.

"What movie?"

"The one with Montgomery Clift."

"I haven't seen that one," I said, disappointed. I liked having my swim suit being compared to Elizabeth Taylor's, and the way Clark was looking at me, I knew it was more than the garment he was admiring.

"*Suddenly Last Summer*, that's it!" he said.

"I never saw it," I said. "But thanks for the compliment."

I hadn't seen the movie. It was like all this stuff just sort of filtered down into my unconscious. Probably from movie magazines which I read voraciously.

Back home, I removed the tags and laid the clothes out on the bed. It was one-thirty and Damion wasn't coming to pick me up until six. I heard a car pull in.

"Nick's here!" Mom called. I felt sick inside. I waited for him to come to the door, but he just sat outside in the car.

"Well. Aren't you going out to say hello?" Mom asked. I hesitated. "What's going on, Margaret?" she asked.

"Nothing." I slipped out the door. Easier to face Nick than Mom when she got that tone of voice.

❖   ❖   ❖

I couldn't believe how I felt about Nick. I essentially felt the same way about him now that I did about Clark. There was no chemistry whatsoever. And that upset me because I could remember, without experiencing the emotion, I could recall how much I had felt for Nick, how much I had adored him, how deep our connection had seemed to be, how he could set fire to me, and woo me, and make me feel all warm and good inside. And suddenly that was dead, just dead and gone.

And that saddened me, left me feeling bewildered and grief-stricken and confused. And angry because it meant that Richie had reached out across the miles (we'd heard that he'd moved back to Winnipeg) and across the years and damaged this pure and precious relationship, my great chance for happiness four whole years after the abuse had ended. If it were not for my fear of being victimized , my need for a sort of super-hero man, it wouldn't have mattered to me if Nick had cried. We might have a troubled relationship, but I would still love him.

I knew that it was my attitude that was responsible for this crashing denouement of my romance with Nick, but I also believed that to respond otherwise was to put myself at risk.

I cannot explain how. I wasn't afraid of being raped in a park or out in the woods at night. Strangers inspired no fear in me. Like most victims of sexual abuse, it was being home that was scary, and in the homes of friends and family.

Besides, I was big girl now with a lot of unresolved anger. I felt I could handle myself. Probably a very foolish notion, but one I held, nonetheless.

CHAPTER 29

I needed protection, I needed a man who was stronger than I was. Did I mean angrier? Eventually that was what I married. But in the meantime, I was still dealing with symptoms and memories the abuse had introduced into my Asperger's world.

From age eleven, from the first moment a sex act was forced on me, I knew it had nothing to do with love or interpersonal relationships. I knew instinctively it was about control. I knew this disgusting old man (Richie must have been all of 36) who claimed to love me had no such feelings for me and never would. I knew he stalked me not because I was beautiful and fascinating but because I wasn't and therefore, no-one would believe me. I knew he didn't want me, Margaret Jean, but my female body. I also knew that the disbelief of my family with regard to the French kissing episode gave him the courage to continue to use me to assauge his perverted appetites. He was a predator with no fear, and I was his target.

Due to these factors, I presented a number of symptoms, the main one being hypervigilance, triggered both by an overwhelming sense of betrayal by my family, and the certain knowledge that no matter where I might be, I could not be entirely sure I was safe. So a new attribute was added to all my Asperger's symptoms: a fact-based fear closely resembling paranoia.

Hypervigilance is a medical term long associated with child abuse and more recently associated with Post Traumatic Stress Disorder in soldiers and policemen. And in fact, the best way I can think of to describe the feeling is to relate it to a soldier who is in a bunker near a sniper. You see, until Richie finally moved away, I had no idea when he would strike or where. I had to be always on alert, constantly on look-out. There was no other soldier to take the next shift. It was always me, always my responsibility and when he caught me unawares, it was my fault. I had failed in my mission to avoid him. He had outsmarted me. That made me dumb. Stupid. A stupid little girl.

I might turn a corner in the yard and find him there waiting for me, or feel completely secure in my home, only to awake and find him, hand clapped over my mouth, beside my bed in the darkness. Take for instance one night when my Mom and Dad were over at his cabin at a party.

❖   ❖   ❖

I was eleven or twelve years old. I don't remember the occasion. It might have been just a good excuse for drinking, singing and dancing and then at the end of it all, the inevitable arguments and brawls. Richie made potato champagne and maybe it was the grand opening of the first bottles. At any rate, Mom and Dad were across the yard in Richie's cabin, and I could tell by the hooting and hollering and carrying on that there was a lot of booze. Dad wouldn't quit drinking for at least another year yet, so he was good and gone for the night. Mom wasn't much of a drinker so she would probably try to sneak home early. Grams was in her bed in the middle bedroom, off the living room, her hearing aid turned off and carefully placed on her bedside table. I was responsible to look after Scotty who would have been about a year old and Terry, who was three. Scotty's crib was in Mom and Dad's room, so until they got home, I was stationed to sleep in their bed, by his crib.

Darkness slithered into the room and settled into the nooks and corners. I pulled the covers up around my ears and reminded myself that I was safely tucked into Mom and Dad's bed. I took a mental inventory: the front and back doors were locked. I was not alone in the house--Grams was there and my little sister, Terry was fast asleep in the bottom bunk in the back bedroom, and my baby brother, Scotty was fed, changed and sleeping peacefully at the foot of Mom and Dad's bed in his crib. I had done everything I could to be safe. Still, uneasiness gnawed at me as I pulled the covers tight, and finally convinced myself it was safe to close my eyes.

Just as I was drifting off to sleep, I heard a sound. Close by. Too close. With a start, I realized it was the window jamb sliding up behind the roller blind. I was suddenly alert, wide awake and breathing hard.

A leg swung over the sill. I sat up immediately and called, "Who's there?" as loud as I could without screaming. And suddenly Richie was in the room. I was scrambling, fighting my way out of the clinging blankets. In one swift step he was at my bedside. Before my feet could hit the floor, his hand clamped over my mouth. His face was so close to mine in the darkness, I could see the gleam of unholy anticipation in his eyes. "Don't scream, or I'll have to hurt you," he said, pressing his hand so hard against my mouth and face I couldn't breathe. "And you know I can," he added. As if it was necessary. He and Dad had been in some barroom brawls and I'd heard many renditions of Richie's role in the fracases.

But more than that, my fear was for Scotty. It honestly never occurred to me then that he might sexually assault Scotty. Those types of stories were considered even more shameful than mine and were seldom released to the public. At age eleven, I knew nothing of them. No, my fear for Scotty was that he would wake up and start to cry and Richie would have to silence him. So I nodded. I would not scream.

He removed his hand. And then he reached under the covers. Furious, I struck out at him. He caught my hand and chuckled as I tried to punch him with my other hand. In one big hand, he caught and held both of mine, forcing my arms back above my head. After that, he took his time, and I realized I'd made a big mistake. Just as when he had kissed me, my resistance seemed to set off some kind of exhilarating electric charge in him. He stayed a long time, and then finally, after what seemed like hours, I heard a key in the back door and heard the door swing open. Richie grinned and raised his eyebrows, "Goodnight my love," he whispered, kissing me on the forehead and making a hasty exit out the window.

"Dad?" I called out even as Richie's one leg was still over the sill.

"No, it's me," said Mom. I heard her go into the bathroom, then the flush of the toilet, the sound of water running in the sink. I heard her go into the kitchen, get a drink of water. I lay there, utterly defeated, demoralized, feeling like scum, like every shred of decency had been ripped from my body. Finally I got up and made my way into my own bed.

I didn't speak to mom, who was rinsing out her glass in the kitchen sink, and I was relieved that she didn't say anything to me. In the first place, I did not for one moment think that she would believe me, and in the second, ironically, I had this notion that I had to protect her from all of this, that Mom's world was good and decent and wholesome, and I would just dirty it up with telling her. Weird, I know, but that's how I felt.

CHAPTER 30

So I knew there was no one to look out for me. For some reason or other, I thought Dad would blame me. And I wanted to protect Mom from the horrible dirty truth about her neighbour. So where could I turn?

Richie's ongoing ability to terrorize me was a constant source of mental anguish. At age eleven and twelve, a slight, unpopular child, I could not reconcile his attentions with my physical reality. And yet, I felt in some way responsible, as if I had "attracted" him. Me: the skinny kid in the home movies with the Afro home-perm hairdo in 1957 before anyone even knows what an Afro is; the skinny kid with bleeding heels because the black and white saddle shoes are too wide for her narrow feet and the blisters haven't healed up yet. The skinny kid with hand-me-down clothes from the Empress laundry.

I had no illusions about my attractiveness. I was not popular with boys my age, or even teenage boys, so I knew Richie's attentions had nothing to do with the usual boy-girl attraction.

Not knowing what had made him zero in on me, I couldn't figure out how to render myself so unappealing that he would leave me alone. I pretty much felt that I was already at rock bottom in the unappealing category.

Not that it bothered me. At age ten I liked to play in the hills and the woods, to build fairy and pixie and elf houses and pretend that they came at night and lived in the homes I had constructed for them. I liked the woods and the trees and flowers that grew along mossy hillsides. I found a perfect peace in nature, and often envied David of Biblical times his shepherding.

I was not concerned about what boys thought, about how I looked to others. I was smart enough in school and liked to read quietly alone, or pump myself way up on the rope swing and sing my lungs out. At ten my appearance was the least of my worries. At eleven, as Richie's chosen target, I found it a puzzlement I couldn't resolve.

And thinking this through, I realized that when my aunts had in his presence refused to believe me when I told them of his first approach, they had made me an easy target. And the horror was that I would continue to be his victim until someone believed me.

This created a tremendous resentment in me for the adults in my family. I had no use for them whatsoever. But outright disrespect would be severely punished, so I bit my tongue and minded my manners, all the while despising them as they played cards with Richie, went out drinking with him, and had him over for dinners and parties.

I felt like the black threes in canasta—a throw-away card. In the whole deck of cards, the black three is worthless, only good for discarding. That was me. Expendable. Good to get off your hands.

CHAPTER 31

Damion was picking me up at four thirty and by three forty-eight, I was standing by the front door watching for the sleek black rental car. The phone rang. Panic seized me—was it Damion to say the party was off? He couldn't pick me up? There was some mistake and I wasn't actually invited? With trembling, perspiring hands, I picked up the receiver. "Hello?"

"Hi, Marg." With relief I realized it was Jillian. "You're still coming to get me, right?"

"As soon as Damion gets here, we'll head over to your place," I assured her.

"Okay. I thought so, but Mom wanted me to double check. So, see you then."

Grams came into the hallway. "Are you going out, dear?"

"Mm hmm. Beach party with the film crew."

"Oh, that's nice dear. My sister used to like the beach. In California, you know. She used to sit in the willows and weave baskets."

Fat lot I cared. I tried to look interested for Grams' sake. I did love her. But honestly, sitting in the bushes weaving baskets? "Oh, are those baskets you have in your room some of hers, then?" Taking a conversational stab in the dark.

"No, no. Those were made by the Indians up on the Nut Lake Reserve."

"Oh. Nice."

Grams cradled her cup of tea in her hands. "Well, I'd better go lie down now. I've been out in the garden and it's played me out."

I looked at Grams, shorter than me, thrifty, hard working. All the women in our family were hard-working. Grams was a widow. Her life became infinitely easier the day her husband died. I've been told he was a cantankerous, diabetic, alcoholic, but from what I remember? The sharp tongue and impatient manner were Gram's hallmarks.

I have great memories of my grandfather; climbing up the hill behind our house with him, me so little I could scarcely see over the Oregon grape bushes. He used to call me "little wee" because I was so thin and tiny. He'd lift me up on the saw-horse when he was cutting wood, the lantern swinging as the saw moved back and forth spewing sawdust, the night insects fluttering by.

He smelled of leather and cigar smoke and sandalwood soap, and I absolutely adored him. He'd take me by the hand and give me a tour of his rose gardens and let me eat peas out of the pods or cucumbers off the vine. I was just six when he died. I loved him dearly. Mom often said I was the only one in the family who did.

Since his demise, Grams had money for pretty clothes, trips to California and even plastic surgery on her nose. She went out with friends to the Canadian Club and afternoon teas and other social events. I wondered how long Dad would live now that he'd quit drinking.

My thoughts were interrupted by the sound of a motor vehicle entering the drive. Damion was early. I smiled. I liked that he was as anxious as I to make this rendezvous. I pecked at Grams' cheek and ran for the door. "Bye, Grams. Gotta go!"

CHAPTER 32

The blare of transistor radios met us as we walked down the beach, Damion staying close beside me, but not taking my hand. Jillian saw some people she knew, and lingered to say hi and chat.

As Damion and I continued down the beach, I saw a bonfire and several of the cast and crew. Damion made a point of introducing me to the people who were in scenes that did not include me, and as we approached an older couple down the beach I was startled to see it was none other than the former Belmont High Drama Teachers, Mr. & Mrs. Ducaine.

How perfect! I thought, trying hard to keep a calm demeanour, as Damion introduced me. We exchanged greetings, Mrs. Ducaine's wispy red hair blowing in the sea breeze, her glasses dangling from their jewelled chain.

I wanted to say, "Oh, I thought you died," or something equally rude but I just couldn't. Instead, I made a cordial reply.

"Do you know each other?" Damion asked. I nodded. I did know the Ducaines.

And now, here I was, face to face with them at a film set party.

"So you had a part in this little film, did you dear?"

"Yes, actually, I did."

"And what was that?" she tilted her head like a bird, smiling.

"The female lead." I said. The smile froze on her face. Damion took my hand and put it through his arm, and said, "Nice to see you." And steered me down the beach.

We wandered along the shore stopping to chat to people here and there. A bonfire smoldered, as if gathering up courage to burst into flame. There were coolers of beverages and hot dogs and hamburgers, potato salad, all the usual picnic fare. Damion kept walking until we rounded a point, and the beach beyond was empty. Then he turned, laced his hand through mine, and kissed me.

The beach did not whirl around me, did not cascade into a thousand little bursts of light, and the earth did not shake beneath my feet. But when

I reached up to touch his face, my hand trembled and my voice when I tried to tell him we shouldn't was simply gone, non-existent, not responding as if my very vocal chords were under his spell when my mind was not.

We walked a little further, and then someone hollered down the beach and I thought of Nick and I wished with all my heart he had told me off, or that I was different, that I could respond differently to male vulnerability.

❖ ❖ ❖

CHAPTER 33

In spite of my parents', neighbours', friends' and sib-
lings' protests, I continued to see Frank the entire
summer of my thirteenth year, 1960. Scarred, tat-
tooed and a complete social misfit, Frank was just
my type. But if I was honest with myself, I had to
admit that he scared me, if only just a little. His
tough-guy look softened when he kissed me, but
he wasn't always kissing me. Sometimes bantering
back and forth and just in general conversation he
could get mean.

And he was strong, physically far stronger than
I was, a fierce fighter unlike Eddy. But everyone's
efforts to dissuade me from seeing him were to no
avail. Frank understood and believed me about
the abuse, and his outrage was a vital component
of my healing process.

And then one day, I was over at Eddy's asleep
in the back seat of the old caddy. It had leather

seats that warmed up nicely in the sun and when I was exhausted from school, sports, housework and homework, I would sneak over to Eddy's and he'd slip into the house, get the keys and unlock the car for me. I'd slide in, curling up against the warm leather.

Eddy would then check if I wanted the windows down or up, make sure I was comfortable, and lock the door so no meandering predators could come and accost me. It was perfect, and of course, I could have simply exited the car any time I wished.

But the drill was that when I woke up, I'd beep the horn and then and only then, Eddy would come and unlock the car with his key.

It's hard to explain today, after Betty Friedan and Gloria Steinem, how terribly important it was in those days for a man to be a man, to be the one who felt he held a woman's safekeeping in the palm of his hand, that he was the watcher at the gate and the keeper at the door and, yes, I suppose the knight in shining armour. To be a man was everything to a boy then, and in order to be so, that was a gift only a woman could give him, and that was the offering I gave Eddy when I called him with the tap on the horn, when I did not reach up and unlock the doors myself.

It was a gift we rarely received and almost never gave—the gift of trust, utter and complete. The gift of making oneself completely vulnerable in the knowledge that we could.

So, once awake, I would arrange myself, my wrinkled skirts and my hair, while he unlocked and opened the car. Then he'd stand leaning on the door, chatting me awake. It was a pleasant and safe ritual and without fail, I slept like a rock.

But this day I woke to the sound of the key turning in the lock. Even before my eyes flew open, fear grabbed my gut and squeezed hard. I jolted awake, rolling over to face the door, pushing myself to a sitting position at the same time, my heart slamming like a hammer in my chest, and by then Frank was halfway in the car. Frank with his intense black eyes and his always just-beneath-the-smiling-surface, deep-seated rage. "Move over," he ordered, sliding onto the seat, giving me a shove on the butt.

I moved, but I was seeing him differently. Eddy had never intruded on me in this way. And Frank seemed angry about something, and instinctively I felt that angry, Frank was dangerous. He reached for me and I pulled away from him. It was an involuntary movement, an intuitive reaction. Uncalled for.

"Now what?" His eyes went flint hard in a split second. "What? You're afraid of *me* now?"

My mouth opened but no words came out.

"This is me." He jabbed his chest. "Frank." I nodded dumbly. "You got nothing to be scared of, Okay?" He said it like it was a test or something.

I nodded again.

"So come here," he said testily.

I hesitated. And even as I did I knew it was the wrong thing to do. So I said quickly, against the flash of anger in his eyes, anger at the mistrust he read in mine, I said, "Give me a chance to wake up. Geez!" and I laughed a little like it was no big deal and I crept over to him and he grabbed me by the arms, hard, bruising me, his fingers pressing deep into my flesh.

And what I wanted was to explode out of there like a shell out of a shotgun, but I knew I had to stay to survive and it felt so much like Richie all over again, so much like I was like eleven years old again and afraid and trying to hide it.

But I went to him, trying to bury my head in his chest so he couldn't see my face until the fear and distrust left my eyes, until I could get with Frank's agenda, whatever it was. But he held me off. Made me look at him. Studied my face.

I didn't cry. I just froze. I wanted to melt into his arms, I knew it was what he needed, but instead I just sat there frozen, my arms throbbing in his grip. And then he realized how hard he was squeezing me, knew I hadn't cried out in pain only because fear had kept me silent. Fear of him. And he released me.

I rubbed my arms with trembling hands, tears in my eyes, crying for what we had lost even before it was completely gone, and I could hear the front door of Eddy's house, hear the creak as it opened and the bang as it swung shut again and Eddy hollering, "Where the f_____'s the keys?"

And I knew he was really upset, because Eddy never swore, and I knew in that moment that as much as Frank understood, Eddy was the one who really knew me.

And Frank looked disgusted and said, "What's with you two?" and he got up out of the car, threw the keys at Eddy, and lit out down the driveway, cursing under his breath, his legs carrying him away on long, urgent strides.

And Eddy was scrambling trying to find the keys in the grass and the dirt, yelling for Frank to come back. I just stood there and watched him go.

❖ ❖ ❖

Around Christmas I got a call that Frank was back in jail. Picked up on a vagrancy charge which meant no money and no place to go. Ended up in the psych ward. Slashed his wrists, Merry Christmas.

I wanted to go see him but I was only thirteen and no-one would drive me and my neighbor Mr. S. said, "He didn't mean to kill himself, my dear. He just wanted to be somewhere warm, where he'd get fed for Christmas. That's all that's about."

And I thought how sad it is when the scars inside you are so bad they start to show on the out-side. And I wished I hadn't been afraid of him in the caddy that day. I knew it was Richie I was afraid of, not Frank, but the two became so interchangeable in that moment, when I heard the key click in the caddy door, when the barricades between me and harm were breached and I was vulnerable.

And I knew then that I was still Richie's victim, even though he lived hundreds maybe thousands of miles away, and not just me, but Frank, too, and where it would stop, I couldn't say, I didn't know, I just sat down and cried, for me, for Frank, for all the wounded children in the world who were trapped in the fear that had been sowed and fostered within their vulnerable souls, the fear that kept them from knowing peace, from finding love, from being whole.

CHAPTER 34

Frank was shipped off to Brannon Lake or the BC Pen, or Okallah, devoured in the maw of an institutional maze. We'd broken up before he left, anyway, and the relief that I'd felt in his presence was short lived.

I was not a delinquent. On the contrary, I was a church-going, law-abiding, more or less well behaved child. Until 'After Frank'. His empathy opened some kind of door inside of me, and some kind of hell let loose, manifesting itself on the written page as foul-mouthed vituperative full-blooded bitchiness. I had a little black suitcase and everything I wrote, poetry, journals, and general rants, I kept locked inside, in the back of my closet buried under the general malaise of teenage closet syndrome.

Since no-one in the real world would listen to me, I expressed everything I ever felt on paper, raging, cursing, crying out to the universe about the injustice of being ignored, dismissed, and in my mind, completely neglected. I wrote explicitly about my experiences with Richie in stories where some psycho teenage delinquent hacked him to pieces or shot him or just plain beat him to death, and then rode off into the sunset on a Harley.

By this time, I was taking nerve tonic prescribed by our family doctor. I had constant, severe head-aches, and trouble sleeping. I had always had high marks in elementary school; the early grades were so easy for me. But now, in grade eight, my assignments were often incomplete, and though I had never been caught playing hooky by either my parents or teachers, the number of days absent recorded on my report card sent a strong message that something was amiss.

My father dreaded teenagers. He often spoke about gangs and gang warfare, about disobedi-ence and insolence in teens. Elvis Presley, jokingly referred to as "Elvis the Pelvis", was increasingly popular. His records were banned in our home, as in others. The arrival of Elvis on the music scene, along with rock and roll, was considered by my father to signal the beginning of the corruption of youth which would lead to the apocalypse— the end of the world. No denomination was responsible for this belief: my parents hadn't darkened a church interior in years. My father didn't believe in letting others interpret the Bible to him. Like his father before him, he preferred to take in its meaning from his own literal translation.

My brother, Rob, being the oldest of us children bore the brunt of this paranoia. He quit school at fifteen, after being described by his Socials Studies teacher, Miss Hughes, as "a lump in the back of the classroom". He tried to get work, but jobs were scarce, even for grown men with families to support, and Dad had a rule: you go to school or you work, but there is no free room and board for a loafer. And when Rob couldn't get work, he had to pack up his few things and leave.

My brother had never been lazy. For at least two summers previous to leaving school, he had worked on a cousin's ranch in the interior. At home, he raised prize-winnings rabbits, a calf, and always helped out. He had a right, a first-born son's right to be with us, to be cherished, to be acknowledged. Instead, he was told to get out and come back when he was man enough to stand on his own two feet.

All of us kids cried the day he left. Scotty sat on the front stoop and waved, tears streaming silently down his two year old cheeks as Rob's old car bumped its way along the rutted gravel drive, paused at the gate, and then turned right onto Station Road and disappeared into the distance. I ran into my room and sobbed. After awhile a knock came at my door. "Time to set the table, Margaret," Gram's voice summoned me. Who felt like eating, I wondered.

The months went by, and one night when dad was getting ready to go out he came storming out to the kitchen, red faced and blustering, holding a white shirt out in front of him like a red rag to a bull. "Whose shirt is this, that's what I want to know!" he demanded.

Mom blanched, looked the shirt over, then sighed. "Well, if it doesn't fit you, then I guess it must be one of Rob's."

Dad's face reflected the processing of this information. Ever one to cheat himself, he never ceased to suspect our faithful mother of having affairs.

We all breathed easier when he laid the shirt across the back of a chair and said, "Well, keep it out of my closet."

"I'll keep it. In my room," I said. "That way it can't get mixed up with Dad's stuff." This made sense, and I got my wish. I had my big brother's shirt.

I loved that shirt. At least two sizes too big, the shirt went perfectly over my jeans. It was considered cool then, to wear a man's shirt over jeans or a pencil skirt, and I felt close to my brother when I wore it.

We weren't close. He was three years older than I, and when I started high school in grade seven, and he was in grade ten, the first thing he said to me was "Don't talk to me in school. I don't want anyone to know you're my sister."

But he could be nice, too. He owned an old truck with a wooden box on the back, his first car, and it meant the world to him. He'd bought it with money he'd earned working away on a friend's ranch in the summer time, before he left home. And one day, in a fit of rare generosity, he decided I could learn to drive.

Trembling, I climbed up beside him on the bench seat.

He showed me the gears, the clutch, the brake. "You don't have to worry about any of those things," he assured me, "You're just going to drive a little way, so all you have to do is steer, and when you want to stop, just step on the brake." Again he showed me the brake. "Okay?"

I nodded, "Okay!"

"Now take your foot off the brake, slowly now, that's right," as I eased my foot off the brake. We were on a bit of an incline in the yard, and I didn't need to press the gas pedal to go forward. The truck began to roll forward. I had a straight clear path ahead of me—all the inner yard, and other than a few minor ruts, nothing to worry about. Rob was pleased as punch with his role of generous older brother, and I was pretty happy being his sister right about then.

But as I cruised along, I began to have serious doubts. This was too easy. Why, it couldn't possibly be this easy to drive a car. If it was, why would driving be reserved for adults and big teenagers? I was rolling along nicely no problem, and I was only twelve for heaven's sakes. And then it dawned on me. It *couldn't* be this easy. It was hard. Somehow, it had to be difficult. Challenging.

Then I realized—of course. I hadn't had to steer yet! Now, if it was easy and anyone could do it, you would just move the steering wheel whichever way you wanted to go. So if it was hard and only adults could do it, you must have to move the steering wheel the *opposite* direction to where you wanted to go.

A large tree stump loomed to the right. I was well clear of it, but just to be on the safe side, I'd better steer around it. Pleased with myself for having figured out the complexities of driving, I turned the wheel to the right. Rob was talking to his friend, Garry, who was sitting in the back.

"Whoa!" Garry hollered, seeing the stump approaching over Rob's shoulder. Too late, Rob turned around just as the truck collided with the stump. The truck sputtered and whined and ground to a sickening halt.

"What the heck?" My brother could not believe what he was seeing and hearing. "What were you thinking?" he demanded, his hands balled into fists at his side. "What the hell were you doing?" He kicked the dash in frustration.

I sat there, speechless at my own foolhardiness. I had totally and completely ruined what could have been one of the best moments in my entire life. I started to cry.

"All you had to do was drive straight!" Rob threw his hat down on the ground and jumped on it, he was so mad.

Rob tried to be an amazing brother, he really did. But the cards were stacked against him.

We slept in rooms at the end of the back hall-way—Rob in a room he shared with the freezer and the washing machine, me in a converted porch I shared with my sister, Terry. The back hallway that led from the back door past our bedrooms had two steps up to the kitchen and I used to run hell bent for leather up those stairs to the bathroom (which was inconveniently located at the other end of the house) in the middle of the night. The pounding of my feet in full gallop always woke Rob up. I think I was about ten when he figured out that if he could break me of the habit of running, if he could some-how make me walk down the hallway, he could get a good night's sleep.

"Marg, could you just walk to the bathroom at night?"

"No."

"Why not?"

"Because. It's dark."

"So?"

"So. It's scary, okay?"

"So turn the hall light on."

"The hall light switch is in the kitchen." I pointed out the obvious.

"So?"

"So how can I walk that far in the dark?" I was thinking of the monsters that lived under my bed. Optimum speed was required to bypass them and make safe passage to the far end of the house. Walking up the hallway, then stopping to turn a light on was a risk I was not about to take.

A few days later he tried another tack. "Just don't drink so much water at night!" he said.

"But I'm thirsty."

"It won't hurt you. You'll just go to sleep and wake up in the morning without having to run to the bathroom all night."

"But I'm thirsty. When you're thirsty it's because your body needs water and you *need* to have a drink."

"It's just one glass of water. It won't kill you to skip it."

"It won't kill you if I drink it, either, will it?" I asked and slammed my bedroom door on him.

Having exhausted the normal course of action, Rob decided to take matters into his own hands. Late one night after everyone was in bed, he set a trip rope across the top of the steps from the back hallway into the kitchen. Once I tripped and fell, I would slow down and walk for sure. According to Rob.

In the wee hours of the morning, I could resist the urge to go no longer. In spite of my fears, I leapt out of bed, flew to the light switch by my door, and took off down the hallway like an Olympic hurdler. I flew up the stairs, clearing the top step by a good two feet, pounding my way to the bathroom.

While I was in the bathroom, I heard a commotion out in the hallway. Coming out as the toilet flushed, I heard Dad say, "What's all the racket out here?" And then, "You fell down? How did you manage that?" And then I saw my brother sprawled on the floor, grabbing his ankle, his face contorted in pain.

"It's all Margy's fault!" he sputtered. "She runs down the hallway every night waking me up. I got up to tell her to be quiet and I tripped and hurt my ankle."

"Is that a string across the hall?" Grams peered out, her silver hair falling gracefully over one eye.

"Oh, never mind," Rob growled.

I started to giggle.

"Oh shut up!" Rob said.

"You kids better get to bed now," Dad said, a smile tugging at the corners of his mouth.

So that was my big brother. No love lost there, right? But I had seen him suffer. Early Sunday mornings, we'd find him sitting with his fishing rod on a stump in the back yard, his face ashen and sullen. Those were the days when Dad was supposed to take him fishing. The problem was Rob couldn't wake up that early. Uncle Steve came to get Dad about four or five o'clock in the morning. In spite of Steve's exhortations for Dad to wake the boy,

Dad had insisted that if Rob couldn't wake up on his own, he didn't deserve to come.

And every time Rob would wake up just as the car doors slammed shut and the engine revved down the drive. He'd leap to his feet, grab his gear, his heart in his mouth, hoping, always hoping that maybe this once, and run like hell. Maybe this time Dad would put on the brakes and wait, or impossible dream! even reverse back down the driveway to pick up his son.

But, no. Rob would run out just in time to watch the tail lights disappear down the road.

So I loved him. I loved him even if he didn't know how to love me.

And wearing his shirt? It made me feel close to him. Like he knew how much I hurt for him, how much I missed him, like we were really brother and sister, caring about each other even if we couldn't be together any more.

CHAPTER 35

One day after Rob was gone, I came home from school to find my mother sitting at the kitchen table with her lips pursed and her eyes sad. Grams was there, too. And my black case, the one with all my writing in it, was set smack dab in the middle kitchen table. My heart froze. Then began to beat in slow, sludge-like beats.

"I take it this is yours, Margaret." My mother said.

"Yes," I said. Everyone knew it was.

"Your father will be home soon. You're to go to your room until then."

I reached for the case. "Uh uh," Mom said. "That stays here."

In my room, I searched frantically for my brother's shirt. I wanted to comfort myself with it, wrap myself in the folds of him, feel as if I had some support in my own home. After tearing apart my closet, my drawers and checking under my bed, I realized it must be in the laundry. I flopped down on the bed and crossed my arms behind my head, wondering what punishment awaited me, and if it meant going without dinner, too.

Hours later, I heard Dad's car in the drive. Heard the car door slam shut, the business-like beat of his footsteps coming to the door, heard him enter, clear his throat and head up the hallway into the kitchen. Low voices. Then Dad's "Well, for heaven's sakes!" Disappointed. Angry.

There was some activity then. I thought they would summon me from my room, but they didn't. I lay quietly on my top bunk wondering what hell I was in for this time. The belt across my legs for sure. I had been dealt that punishment before. We all had, Terry maybe being the exception. It wasn't so bad. As Mom was fond of saying, the belt left no scars and you lived through it.

I waited. The night grew dark. After awhile I smelled wood smoke and looking out my window, noted sparks drifting into the night sky.

Someone flung open my door. Dad stood there, imperious, his face stiff with anger. "You can come out here with us and watch." It was a command, not a suggestion. I moved out into a night lit up by the ragged flames of a bonfire slicing into the darkness of the yard, They had set it up on the hard-packed earth between the garage and the chicken coop. Fear rippled through me, playing nervously on my intestines.

I walked slowly over to the fire. My grand-mother stood there, her face hard against me. Terry and Scotty stood back from the edge of the fire. I was thirteen, so Terry was five and Scotty was three.

My father spoke. "I'm very disappointed in you, Margaret. Writing filth like this. You know better. You've been baptized in the Lord and this is what you come up with! You're on the road to Hell, and we are here tonight to save you."

While I stared uncomprehendingly at him, he opened my little suitcase. White pages with hand-writing in blue fountain pen ink fluttered in the firelight. "These are the work of the devil," he said grimly. And with a flick of his wrists and a twist of his arm, he shook the case toward the fire, pages wafting down into the flames. I opened my mouth to speak. And then closed it.

They hadn't read anything I'd written, really. They must have seen the four letter words and just stopped reading. Because if they'd read every-thing, they'd know, and they'd be reaching out to me, wanting to comfort me, wanting to know if

I was alright, saying they were sorry and saying *if they'd only known*...

The fire crackled. The smoke made my eyes tear up.

There was some good poetry in there, too. Poetry Clark and I had critiqued, stuff I was working on. I watch the flames devour it line by line. Part of me, gone forever. The deepest, truest part of me.

And then my mother handed something off to Dad. Dad held it up so I could see, see the collar and cuffs, the whiteness, the purity of it, the shirt that meant everything in the world to me. And with a triumphant smirk he tossed it into the fire.

I nearly dove in after it. I can't really say what stopped me. It wasn't fear of pain because by then I felt absolutely nothing. Nothing at all. I watched the fire devour the shirt, blackness overtaking the bright whiteness of the garment, watched the edges of the fabric curl, and turn to black cinders, some of which drifted aimlessly up into the night.

I watched it all like a film reel, Terry staring wide-eyed at my shirt as the flames raced along the edges. Scotty wiping tears with small fists, his eyes dark against pale cheeks, a small child frightened at the unanticipated violence of his sister's clothes burning, stealing glances at our father as if afraid to look and yet unable to look away, as if that man had been transformed: a monster unveiled.

I wasn't strapped. There was no need. They burned the suitcase last.

CHAPTER 36

There were some logs up ahead and Damion steered me toward them. A few stragglers wandered down the beach toward us and Damion skipped stones and talked about his schedule after the film was done, always keeping an eye toward the others on the beach. And then we were alone again, and with some urgency, he grasped my shoulders and kissed me, the kind of kiss that zooms your heart into an out-of-body experience and sends a thrill of fire through your veins and I forgot about Nick and just surrendered to the moment.

Someone called to us. It was the Ducaines wanting us to come and see some sailboat or kite, and by then he had his arms full around me, and we broke apart, my face red from his four o'clock shadow, and we turned reluctantly back down the beach. My heart singing and my mind afraid of what I might do, I walked back into the small cluster people watching a kite race along the shore. Damion followed a short distance behind.

Jillian caught up to me. "Marg, are you going swimming?" she asked. I saw that she was already in a black swim suit with a pretty cover up and sandals. I'd bought a new suit, so why not.

"Sure," I said. "Where do we get changed?" She showed me, and I found my bathing suit with some other things I'd brought and went and changed.

I knew the swimsuit more than did me justice. It was a one piece—two piece swim suits had just been invented, and believe me, by today's standards the *itsy bitsy teeny weeny yellow polka dot bikini* was a major cover up. Anyway, I waded into the water and swam with Jilly for maybe half an hour. Then the food was up, so we decided to go in.

The sun was setting behind us as we waded out of the waves onto the shore and as we did, an appreciative whistle broke the chatter. Judy blushed and looked at me and grinned. Then suddenly she really blushed. "Omigosh, Marg, you're suit is…well, …it's…"

"It's what?" I asked in exasperation.

"See through!"

I looked down. Dry, it was fine. Wet, it was dicey. Not quite see-through, but every little curve showed. We ran to get our towels, and Damion held his out for me to run into and wrap around me. He didn't dare kiss me in front of Smith and Sydowski, but if anyone on that beach didn't know he wanted to, they weren't paying attention.

Later we ate, and chatted, and then the guitars came out and the singing started. Damion asked me if I knew any songs. Oh Asperger's moment!

Some people with Asperger's have a lesser developed inner ear and cannot properly hear the words to songs, either on the radio or on tape or any other device. I am one of these. The funny thing is, I always think I can. But when I start sing-ing, my friends laugh and say, "Those aren't the words!"

So from my earliest teens I knew how it was with me, and when Damion asked me to name a song I could sing, I honestly felt like an animal prowling around a trap on tip toe, examining it from all sides, trying to think how to avoid getting caught, and still make off with the bait. Only the animal would probably just be wary. I was terrified. Naturally, Damion took my hesitation for modesty.

"I'm sure you must know something," he urged. He named a few songs, me shaking my head, "no" at each. He gave me a look, that same frustrated look every adult gets when they are urging me to cooperate and express myself and I seem to be stubbornly refusing.

I knew the words to the hymns we sang week after week at the little brown Baptist Church, and I was confident I knew them because I read them off the hymn-book page. I'd been reading and singing those songs for at least eight years and I could sing like nobody's business in the pews.

But popular songs were different. And Damion was sitting there, the man who mere hours ago had taken me in his arms and kissed me as if I was succor to his soul now strummed a discordant chord on his guitar and eyed me with exasperation.

"*Down in the Valley*," I said. "I know *Down in the Valley*." It was a simple country ballad, and I felt quite certain of the words. All the same I sang in *sotto voce* so that his words would carry over mine, just in case. To my great relief our voices blended well together and there was quite the applause when we finished.

"That's not the only song you know?" Damion prodded.

I felt as people must when they have just gotten safely to the far side of a land mine field, only to be told they must go back the same way. I had to think of something fast. Something everyone would want to sing, something really popular.

"How about *Love Me Tender*?" I asked. Naturally, Damion knew the Elvis hit, everyone did. Long before the end of the song, the others joined in, and I was safe, their voices overriding mine, echoing over the beach, the susurration of the waves adding to the melancholy of the tune. In time, darkness settled over the scene, and after a while people doused the fire and we bid the stars goodnight.

After we dropped Jillian off, Damion turned to me in the car, ran his fingertips over my hand and said, "Is there someplace we could go?"

My knees nearly melted. I knew lots of places. Nick and I had frequented all of them. But Damion was a man who had by his own admission, slept with a lot of girls, and it was never my intention to be one of a herd. I was still searching for that innate Margaret Jeanness, and I didn't think sleeping with Damion would aid in that endeavour.

And while Nick was a gentleman, an honourable man who would never in a million years go all the way with me out of respect for me and my family, Damion was obviously a tiger of a different stripe, with absolutely no compunction about firing me up and stoking me to a bright white heat. I may have frequented these places with Nick, but I was wise enough to know I couldn't go there with Damion.

"I told my parents I'd be home by midnight and it's nearly that now," I said.

"It's only 11:20. And if you were late, so what?" Damion asked, disbelief registering on his face.

"I'll get in trouble if I'm late." At least it was the truth.

Damion sighed and turned the engine on. "Okay. Time to go home," he said and fired up the car. I sighed. My friends would never believe this either.

When I got home, Dad was waiting up. "You're home early," he said, puzzled and surprised.

"Only a few minutes," I said.

"Did you have a good time?" he asked.

"Hmmhmm. It was great. How were things at Kitty's?"

"Oh we got the job done, alright. It's a good thing he had my saw."

I nodded. "That's good, Dad. Well, I guess I'll go to bed now."

"Well, goodnight then." I slipped back down the hall to the room I shared with Terry, who was sleeping over with our cousins. The room was peaceful in the dark, and I didn't want to turn the light on. Tonight I did not fear the darkness. Tonight I felt powerful, in control. Like that night when I was twelve, and I brought things with Richie to an end all by myself.

CHAPTER 37

It was my idea to join Brownies, the elementary school contingent of Girl Guides, which is the equivalent in Canada of Boy Scouts. As I say, I wanted to join Brownies, but when I was twelve, nearly thirteen, and the time came to graduate to Girl Guides, I'd pretty much had enough of earning badges through crafts and wanted out. However, quitting was something not tolerated in our family, and Mom insisted I continue on.

That's how it came about that I was walking home one early December evening, singing "How Great Thou Art", my favorite outdoors nature type hymn. Walking home from a Girl Guide meeting, alone in the moon-silvered darkness of a winter's night, belting out a hymn along a road with no sidewalks.

The sessions were usually over by five o'clock, but it was late winter and the sun set around four, and by five it was full night. I tended to dawdle a bit, taking in the stars and the moon, all of which seemed to signify in a deeply personal way, God's creative power, heavenly bodies which on this winter night gleamed particularly bright.

And so it happened that I was singing and praying and dreaming along the road when a car turned into the road at the intersection behind me. Caught me in its headlights. Slowed. Pulled up beside me.

I did not want to turn and see who it was. I was afraid I already knew it was the little red car, by the sound of the engine. Already knew the freckled face of the driver. He spoke and my worst fears were realized.

"Get in," Richie grinned from the driver's side window. "I'll give you a lift home."

I kept walking, thinking, praying silently, frantically Oh Lord, oh God, oh Lord Jesus, tell me what to say!

"Margy?" he said, his voice getting sterner. "I said to get in."

I sighed. And then I did something that surprised me. I just stopped walking. I turned and looked at him. And in that moment when I met his slightly protruding blue eyes, his arrogant grin, I knew I could not go on. Not if he beat and tortured me. Not if he killed me. I just could not stand for this to happen to me one more time.

"No, Richie."

He looked at me askance. "We're engaged," he said, invoking this sick and dumb bullshit that he used to rationalize what he did to me.

I looked him right in the eye. I said, "Well, Richie, I think it's time we told Mom and Dad and Andrea what's going on here. Don't you?"

He looked at me as if I had suddenly sprouted facial warts. "What are you talking about?" he asked. For the first time ever he seemed fidgety, nervous.

"Of course Dad will say you're a little old for me, but when I tell him what we've been doing, he'll see right off that I'm old enough."   Where those words came from, I had no idea. I was as surprised to hear them come out of my mouth as he was.

At first he was stunned, as if he couldn't believe his ears. Then, when he realized I meant what I said, (little did he know I would never dream of telling my father), he started squirming in his seat.

"Well, I've been thinking about that, Margy," he said.

"Margaret. My name is Margaret." I interrupted.

"Margaret. You see, I've been thinking maybe I'm a little old for you after all."

257

I nodded. "Me, too."

"Like maybe we should break it off. Stop seeing each other." Perspiration beaded at his hairline and began to creep down his forehead. He tried to smile at me, hoping and praying I would go along with him.

For a moment, I almost didn't. I wanted so badly to tell Mom and Dad what he had done to me. But in the darkness of that night, under the frosted stillness of the stars, I knew in my heart that if Richie denied my accusations, they were more likely to believe him than me, and then I would be his victim forever.

Like the winds of winter, a tremendous sadness swept through my soul, and that sense of complete aloneness, of absolute isolation from all aspects of community soughed through me, and left me bitter and cold. And somehow strong.

"That would be good, Richie. That would be the best thing."

Relief visible in his eyes, he nodded. "Well, alright, then. That's how it is. It'll be our little secret."

Oh, man, how sick that made me feel. *Our **dirty** little secret you mean, you sonofabitch.* But by the grace of God, I kept my calm demeanour. "As long as we don't 'see' each other anymore," I insisted.

"You bet," he said, and without any further ado, shifted as the car accelerated silently into the night, its headlights bleak in the moonlight.

I stood there for a long moment, waiting for him to turn around and come back, but something told me he wouldn't, told me I'd probably never have to worry about him again. Sure enough, shortly after that encounter, he announced he'd put in for a transfer, one that would take him back East.

But that night, when I realized he was really gone, that he would never bother me again, that I had banished him myself, my first reaction was despair. How could it have been that easy? Why didn't I do this before? I despised myself with all of my twelve year old heart.

But then I shook my head. "NO, Margaret Jean," I said. I said it right out loud. "Never mind that rot. This is a victory!"

I belted out "Onward Christian Soldiers" and sent a million prayers of thanks to God in heaven. I laughed, I nearly cried, I hugged myself and then I danced a little jig right there on Station Road. And trembling with joy, I picked up my pack and went home.

CHAPTER 38

The filming ended soon after the beach party. Viewing the film now, I see that the "lead female role" was actually a rather small part, but it provided a big opportunity for me, through Damion. On the set one day, he mentioned that a new theatre group was starting up in Victoria and he and Smith were going to dinner with the founders. Would I be interested in coming along? Damion could introduce me to them and get my foot in the door.

My Asperger's heart was suddenly flooded with anxiety. Waves of uncertainty washed over me. I had never been to a first-class restaurant before. The closest I had ever come was the shipboard dinner during the film, where everything was predetermined, and all I had to do was watch the others to see which utensil to use, how to unfold the napkin and so on. But this was different—this would be strictly off the cuff. And what did one say to people planning to start up a theatre group? Or the more pertinent question for an Asperger's teen—what was the wrong thing to say? Probably just about anything I might blurt out. So trembling slightly, I said to Damion, "I don't know."

Damion did a double take. "You don't know?"

"I've never been to a restaurant like that." Even to me, my excuses sounded lame, but they weren't excuses. Based on my experience, they were *reasons*.

"Look, just watch me. If you have any questions, ask me. It'll be fine," he added, grinning at what he perceived to be my foolishness. I knew I had to agree or Damion would be terribly offended, and so I nodded and said, "Sure." Nevertheless, the generous invitation felt awfully like an invite to walk a tight rope stretched over a mile-high canyon with a pit of snakes squirming hopefully on the rocks below.

Dinner started well. I was not overdressed. But when the waiter pulled out my chair I was already lowering myself into the one next to it. How was I to know high-class girls couldn't get into a chair by themselves?

If everyone else could have ordered before me it would have made the experience much easier for me, I'm sure, but I was the only female present, and thus, I got to order first.

Paul's restaurant, a popular teen hangout that Clark Boswell used to take me to occasionally, had a salad called Crab Louie which I really liked, and it was on this menu. "Aha!" I congratulated myself silently, "This is okay. This I Can Do!" And I promptly ordered the dish.

However, just as I was breathing a sigh of relief, the waiter poised his pencil above his order pad and enquired, "Soup or Juice?"

"Soup or Juice?" I repeated dumbly.

"Yes," Damion said, quick to jump in and explain. "It comes with the meal. You can have your choice of soup or juice."

The soups I'd had the most experience with were bland store-bought tinned soups watered down to serve our large family. What kind of soup might surface in a restaurant I had no idea. But I knew about juice. Apple or orange was occasionally served in four ounce glasses with breakfast at home. So I promptly said, "I'll have orange juice, please."

"Orange juice?" exclaimed the waiter, his well-trained eyebrows nonetheless exhibiting surprise.

"People usually have tomato juice with dinner," Damion explained.

My mind reeled. *Well, if they usually have tomato juice then why didn't the waiter say 'tomato juice'?*

I wondered irritably. Annoyed and embarrassed, I looked Damion straight in the eye and said, "But I always have orange juice with Crab Louie."

Damion bit back a grin. Without missing a beat, the waiter asked, "And what kind of cheese would you like in it?"

Oh my gawd, could they not just serve the salad?

"What kind of cheese do you have?" I asked, hoping to avoid the juice trap.

The waiter listed off several, including "Roquefort", which sounded French, and Clark had told me French cheese was delicious.

"Roquefort," I said decisively.

Damion cleared his throat. "That is commonly called 'blue cheese'," he informed me.

"Blue cheese. Well, blue is my favorite color, you know. That's why I like it."

"The blue is mold," Richard S., unimpressed, supplied this information from across the table.

For a split second I stared at Richard with his silver hair and bored blued eyes. I wasn't seeing or thinking about him, though. I was trying to comprehend the fact that in first class restaurants they served moldy cheese. I gave up. "Of course it is. And that's what I want."

The waiter smirked and nodded and turned to Damion. To my relief, I liked the sharp taste of the blue cheese. In fact, it became one of my favorites.

So I lived through dinner. Mostly I listened attentively the way I did with boys on dates, eyes fastened on the speaker as if they were the only person on earth. It got me through the dinner table conversation without any further gaffs. At least, that I was aware of.

My anxiety level was at maximum and my toler-ance for social groups was almost exhausted when Damion and Smith, Richard S. and his friend Wolf, and I left the restaurant. I had come on my own, so I would drive home in the little turquoise Renault that was my father's current ride; Dad was always buying/selling/trading in cars when he was work-ing and we owned different vehicles all the time. This one was European and sporty and looked well on me as I waved goodnight to everyone.

The sun was just setting when I turned the car right up Douglas Street, away from Langford and toward the seawall on Dallas Road. The pearl grey sky that marked the final fade-out from sunlight into darkness lay across the horizon like rippled silk as I parked the car and stepped out onto the path along the shore.

Waves slapped against the sea wall, gulls hung in the air, their cries piercing the night. Lovers walked in twosomes, holding hands, or arms linked. Nick and I had walked here many times, and remembering how close we had been tinged the night with sadness.

As I strolled out along the headland, I became aware of people partying along the shore—a clinking of bottles, the smoke and flame of bonfires. Muted voices and laughter drifted through the air. Now and then the glowing tip of a discarded cigarette butt arced toward the sea.

The breeze ruffled my hair and brushed my face, and I looked out at the vast undulating emptiness of the sea and felt comfortably isolated from all human activity. Inhaling the salty essence of the sea, I let the night absorb me. I felt my anxieties draining away, peace rippling through me. I felt my shoulders relax, and tilted my head to watch the night sky. I walked a way along the shore, the gravel of the path crunching very satisfactorily in the silence. The sound of the surf soothed me, the regular rhythm of it, the soft susurration of water washing sand. I walked until I felt completely relaxed, until the tension in my neck and stomach were gone, and my mind was at peace.

And then a horn sounded and someone peeled into the parking lot, and I turned and headed back to the Renault.

CHAPTER 39

When it came time for Damion to leave town with the crew, he phoned to see if we could meet one last time. We had been out before, while the filming was still going on, even though my role was done. We had gone to a beach in Sooke, and played on the rocks, a childish game of tag, and lay afterwards, spent, on his jacket on the sand.

I loved being held and kissed. There is just no getting away from that fact. Richie never practiced such love-making arts; his was simply a crude taking of what he wanted, and so I never associated that experience with the more pleasant aspects of what I thought of as "cuddling" and what we all referred to in teen lingo as "necking".

"Necking" at least in my vocabulary, was different to "making out" which implied some sexual foreplay at the very least. Necking was that warm and wonderful embrace where kisses flew like swallows homing in on Capistrano. Nothing to fear there.

Kissing Damion was fine, but I could never forget his age, which must have been close to that of Richie. At least much closer to Richie's than to mine. No matter what I might think of Damion, the age difference made me uncomfortable, and I could not contemplate having the kind of intimate moments I had with Nick, with this older man. So after a few minutes, I drew away from him.

Sensing my withdrawal, he began to talk about all the girls he'd made love to, in Toronto, New York, Montreal. Scads of women. Kazillions. So many he couldn't even remember the names of some of them. He looked at me to see how I was taking in this information.

I grinned and gave him the Adam eyes. "But I want you to remember me," I said.

He smiled. Reached his hand out to mine, and said, "Making love just seems a natural ending for us." He drew me closer.

I leaned into him. "But I want to be certain that you'll remember me." I reached up and traced his lips like I'd seen Sophia Loren do in the movies, "Not just one more face in the crowd, you know?"

He tightened his arm around me, drawing me even closer, and moved my hair out of my eyes.

Put his hand on my cheek. I kissed his hand softly. "Make me remember," he whispered, leaning in.

"You'll remember, me, Damion," I said, leaning in to kiss his neck. "I'm going to be the one," I kissed him again, "who didn't sleep with you." And I pulled away.

He laughed a little, uncertain. Then he drew me to him and kissed me again. I let him, and then I sat back. Our eyes met. Suddenly, he realized I was serious.

I could see him processing this information in disbelief. Then he laughed. "Okay." He said. "Have it your way. But you don't know what you're missing."

I could live with that.

❖   ❖   ❖

As for Nick, well, after the film wrapped up and Damion and I had said our last good-byes, I went up to Golden where Aunt Nell had moved, to baby-sit my cousins for a week.

It was a crushing denouement to my acting career, making Kraft dinner for three younger cousins for lunch, sweeping up and doing dishes and laundry and chasing the dog out of the kitchen. Even going for walks in the muddy flats was no fun. I couldn't go anywhere without wrecking my shoes.

When I got home, the frustration increased. After living an experience few girls my age got to enjoy, I was suddenly stranded back in my old life. And the first thing Mom said to me when I got in the door was that Nick had left me a letter, and I'd better read it because he was calling three or four times a day every day.

After a week in Golden (strictly Nowheresville, believe me) I was ready to see Nick again. "Give me the letter," I said, picturing a small white envelope with a brief note asking if he could see me.

"Just a minute," Mom disappeared into the hall closet and came out carrying what looked to me like a small suitcase, something I would later understand was a briefcase.

"What's that?" I asked, uneasy at the sight of it.

"Nick's letter's in there," Mom said, handing it to me. I felt like I was reaching for a nest of vipers barely contained in a gunny sack. But I took it.

The letter was 13 pages long. Thirteen, that dreaded number that I had hated to say when I was a child. Thirteen pages of densely packed, all caps peckish printing, explaining that we were meant to be together, how it was God's will that I should come back to him, and how he was praying for us to be together again.

I knew he meant well. I knew he had a good heart. And yet, the letter made me sick to my stomach. I couldn't say why. I couldn't even read the whole thing. When he phoned later that day, I took the call reluctantly. He asked me out and I agreed to go. It was what everyone wanted; everyone except his mother and me.

When Nick came to pick me up his eyes were bright, his skin pale and feverish, and his attitude was different. "We always do what you want," Nick told me, "I've spoiled you rotten, and now it's time for a change."

I was stunned. My number one line with men was, "Whatever you want, dear." It worked very nicely since I had very few wants of my own. I went to movies with Jenina occasionally if there was one I wanted to see that Nick didn't, and since I had no hobbies, it was easy to go along with whatever activity Nick had in mind. I had been to ecumenical conferences with him, on hikes and to parties held by his friends and his church. I could not for the life of me remember ever saying what I wanted to do. Poetry reading, jazz clubs, art galleries I reserved for my friendship with Clark. With Clark there was no romantic involvement, so no chance of losing him. I could be myself utterly and completely with Clark, in a way I never could be with any of my boyfriends.

So I just sighed. Nick's Mom must have fed him this line of crap. But okay, I probably deserved it. I would go along. But even as I climbed into the car, the letter lingered in the back of my mind like a dark warning.

Nevertheless, I said, as always, "Whatever you want Nick."

He picked roller skating. Roller skating? I had never been roller skating in my whole entire life. I told him this and he said, "You'll just have to learn won't you?" and when we got to the rink, he put his skates on and took off.

I have to rent a pair of skates. I have to get them on, and then I have to stand up and walk out onto the rink. I get out there and I can barely stand up and every time I try to move forward, my feet start going in different directions and I'm left in the middle! I was terrified, and there's Nick skating around out there like he's a captain in the roller derby.

So when two very nice young men come over and one says, "Whoa! Looks like you need a hand, here" I most graciously accept and they kindly assist me the whole time while Nick is skating in reverse or doing some twirly thing, skating very fast through the crowds while I and my escorts excuse our way along the edge of the rink.

I was not bad by the time Nick said we had to go. I believe if the boys had let go, I could have stood up on my own.

He was truly irate, which was entirely uncalled for, since he wouldn't even help me learn. I was furious. I could not believe he thought abandoning me on the rink was going to in any conceivable way improve our relationship. I didn't get it, and I absolutely did not want to get it.

He didn't even help me untie my skates. He just took his off and strode out to the car. It took me awhile to get my skates unlaced, I was so angry I was trembling, which didn't help one bit. I dropped my skates off at the rental counter and then went out to look for Nick. He was sitting in his car all ready to go. Mad as hell, I marched over to the car.

"What was that all about?" I asked him. He didn't even reach over to open the door for me.

"Get in. We're late for dinner."

"We're through!" I said.

"Fine," he retorted, then added, "You just have to have everything your way, or forget it. Alright. Forget it!" he said and drove off.

275

Relief unexpectedly flooded through me. Of all the emotions I'd expected to feel, relief didn't even make the list. But that was what I felt, and I felt lighter as I walked the few blocks to the bus stop.

❖　❖　❖

"What happened to Nick?" Mom asked.

"We broke up."

"You better think about that," Mom said. "You'll really upset that boy if you don't get back together with him. He's pretty stuck on you."

"Not anymore," I said.

After that he phoned like three times a day. Talked to Mom for hours. She really wanted us to get back together. But I could hardly value her opinion. After all, she was married to Dad.

❖　❖　❖

Margaret Jean Adam

Love is like a red, red rose.
On the surface all velvet and perfume
But underneath there are thorns my sweet thing
And the deeper you go, the more love wounds.

So stay on top of love, my sweet things,
For the deeper that you go,
The more love hurts and the sooner withers
That velvety perfumed red, red rose.

And love is like a slender bottle
Of the most expensive red wine
It's taste so sweet, its colour so tempting
But tomorrow's headache is not so divine.

So just sip at love, my sweet things,
Because the more that you take,
The more that love is gonna hurt you tomorrow
The more your poor heart is gonna ache.

Oh, love is like a red, red rose.
MJ Adam, 1963.

CHAPTER 40

Clark Boswell, my very good friend from Oak Bay, would discuss any subject with me, and in my Asperger's way, I was quite transparent with him.

After Richie, my faith in God became a double-edged sword. I believed in God. I did. But I could not get Dr. Metralkis' words out of my head. I hadn't expected God to swoop down from heaven and save me, but I had expected Him to send some mortal representative to rescue or at least lend support to me. Someone to punish and torture Richie would have been nice.

Clark and I often discussed religion, and he was very supportive. Most of his concern was that I should have whatever moral support I could muster, and he knew I drew a lot from my faith.

But there was a Bible verse that gave me a lot of anxiety. Romans chapter twelve and verse one read:

I beseech you, therefore, brethren, by the mercies of God, that ye present your bodies a living sacrifice, holy, acceptable unto God, which is your reasonable service.

Now, I had no problem with the "sacrifice" part of the quotation. The part that had me worried was "holy". I pointed out to Clark that the word was isolated by commas, meaning that it was a stand-alone condition that had to be met in order to be of service to God. And since I was ruined when I was eleven, there was just no getting beyond the fact that my body had been defiled and therefore was not holy in any regard, and could never be so.

In those days, in the 1950's and 1960's, a woman's virginity, her purity was considered an important source of pride for her family. If you were a virgin, you were entitled to wear white on your wedding day. If you were not, you must wear a dress of a different colour.

Of course, more sophisticated women completely ignored the protocol. They brazenly wore white whatever the circumstances and braved the whispered rumours. But those of us who came from strict lower class families adopted the rules and lived by them.

I knew one thing for sure; Richie had left me anything but pure. Every time I thought about him, I felt dirty and sick. I was not holy.

And it was not my sin to be forgiven, so how did that get cleansed? By the time I began to have these conversations with Clark, my faith had been seriously affected by Dr. Metralkis, and God and religion were all beginning to seem like a moot point anyway.

No one in decent society wanted to talk to me about my issues, and my family hadn't had the money to keep me in sessions with Metralkis for long. Not that I was eager to see her again. So I was left to discuss these issues with my odd assortment of friends.

Clark, an atheist, was adamant that God wouldn't care, and neither would any future husband worth his salt. I was grateful to Clark for that opinion, but I couldn't help wondering, as an atheist, what could Clark really know of God? And I would rather die than bring up the topic with Pastor Moorhouse or his pretty red-haired wife who was six months along with their third child.

The thing was, I needed my faith. I needed to believe that God was watching over me, even if it meant he'd left me alone and unprotected, even if it meant he had stood and watched while I'd been humiliated and shamed, even if it meant he had created Richie as well as me and for some reason unclear to me, loved us both.

I had no other family. I was not connected to my brothers and sister. I was not connected to my parents. I was alone in the universe, except for God and his creations, and the thought of being without him, without his mercy and his love felt not so much terrifying as empty. Completely utterly empty. Void.

That's what was left for me without God. A huge void. A lot of nothingness going on in Margaret Jean here.

Dr. Metralkis had put a serious damper on my faith, and to my way of thinking? St. Paul reached across the centuries to all but extinguish it. In the darkness of the world I now inhabited, my faith flickered and faltered. And I stepped tentatively into the darkness.

God never deserted me. I isolated myself from him by choosing to decide that Richie's sin could exclude me from Christ's circle of grace. Until I could allow myself that grace, I would wander in a wilderness of loss.

CHAPTER 41

September came and I went back to school. People were surprised Nick and I weren't together any-more. I was still in the drama club and he was still the stage manager. Our paths inevitably crossed.

I didn't have a new boyfriend. The theatre group kept me pretty busy. My picture had been in the paper, sewing curtains for the renovated church-theatre, and I might have enjoyed my slight celebrity status except for the fact that it only seemed to isolate me more.

Jenina was still my friend, we still stuck our bare feet in the mud puddles during track practice (shoes weren't such a big deal back then), and we were both on the basketball team. But the nights and weekends were lonely and eventually I gave in to Nick. Or maybe I called him.

My parents were delighted to see him at the door and invited him in for a piece of homemade apple pie and a cup of coffee. Nick declined, saying we had better get going and took me straight out to the beach. We walked for miles, holding hands and talking.

Mostly Nick talked. I was uneasy; I still had no feelings for him, and I just couldn't believe I couldn't bring those feelings back. I felt sick about it, sick at heart, and wondered what the hell was the matter with me. What the kids at school and mom and dad said must be true. I was weird.

Nick was obviously relieved and happy to be with me again. I didn't say anything to counter that. When we got back to the car, he said he had a special place to show me. We drove up away from the beach and down a few remote roads to a secluded, wooded knoll. We parked, and I prepared to get out. Nick let me go, and then came around and stood and admired the view with me. After a few minutes he began to kiss me, more and more passionately. Then he scooped me up in his arms and carried me around to the back seat door, and opening the door, slid me onto the leather seat. Sweat beaded his brow, and he stretched his frame over me, his passion inflaming his kisses, urgency drawing him down on me.

I didn't fight him. I wanted to feel something, anything, to feel connected, to share his passion, but I couldn't. But I told myself, maybe I would if we made love, everything would come back, everything would be good again, and we could be together again, really together. And then he whispered, "We'll be married soon, next year, maybe," and startling even myself, I pushed him up and said, "No, Nick, No. Not married."

And then he said, "Why? I don't understand. Why?"

I shook my head sadly. "I just don't love you anymore."

He stared at me in disbelief. "But you were willing to... I almost... We nearly went all the way. Why, if you don't love me, for heaven's sake, why?"

"I'm just so lonely, Nick," I said.

He got up off me in disgust and sat in the doorway. Neither of us spoke for a few minutes. Finally he stood up and said, "I'd better get you home."

❖   ❖   ❖

I saw him around school, naturally. Every now and then his mother would phone my mother and complain that I had ruined her son, broke his heart, made him crazy with grief. But I couldn't believe her. Nick had been unable to look at me all the long drive home.

❖   ❖   ❖

285

I went back to school feeling adrift in my own life. I was still in drama, of course, and backstage, I studied Nick from afar. I felt nothing, even when he'd put his arm around another girl just to make me jealous.

I still went to church, belting out the hymns every Sunday morning, attending young people's when it didn't interfere with the theatre schedule downtown. But my faith, like my social connections, was no longer bolstered by Nick's gregarious example, and without a guide I faltered, the words of Dr. Metralkis and St. Paul haunting me, calling me to abandon hope.

Perhaps if I'd had those decoder glasses, I could have kept my faith. Because in a way, it was my tendency to rely on the verbal or written word that confused me. I couldn't look at the context of Paul's statements, or take into account the fact that while Dr. Metralkis' background was very different from mine, it did not mean it had more value.

I felt myself becoming more isolated, emotionally and socially floundering. Heading into winter, I found myself feeling alone as a piece of flotsam adrift on a vast and featureless sea.

Yes, I had seized the moment to get the film job, but at sixteen, I had no idea how to follow that up to my advantage, how to break the process down into meaningful steps that might lead to future successes, which could eventually lead to a self-sufficient life.

I was drifting further and further off course, helplessly swept up in a powerful, pulsating current, unable to stop, plant my feet, and take the lie of the land. Without Nick's social navigation, and having disavowed myself of the comforting sense of belonging to God's family, I found myself socially and culturally disconnected.

So there I was, Asperger me, leaving the threshold of that golden sixteenth summer, turning seventeen, all aspiration and complexes, heading out into the world. And I thought about Nick and my mother, and how they seemed remote somehow, you know? Like islands seen from the shore, a geographical certainty and yet an unknown, viewed without any sense of familiarity. And I thought about the mists that shroud the islands and I knew it was not like that with Mom and Nick; it was too much knowing.

Familiarity breeds contempt Grams used to say. Is it always so? I wondered. How could it be if people fell in love and married and stayed together to raise families, have friends, and take their place in the church and the community? How could familiarity breed contempt? This proverb did not soothe me at all, did not make me feel at ease about the coldness in my heart.

Instead, I felt anxious, as if I were withdrawing from the great circle of life, of friends and family. Would I be frozen out, alone and unloved? If so, it would be my own fault, because I could not do what Christ bade us do.

We were taught to pray *forgive us our trespasses as we forgive those who trespass against us.* We made this covenant every time we intoned the Lord's Prayer: at school, at church, at Young People's. In order to be forgiven, we must first forgive.

And if Nick and Mom were metaphorical islands, surely I was an iceberg. How could I expect salvation, Asperger me? Heartless. Empty. Unforgiving.

CHAPTER 42

*I was in the gym only it was all backwards the gym floor
was raised and the stage was by the door and lower
and I was on the gym part with torn curtains burgundy
velvet high up and flapping from floor to ceiling and it's
dark in there like nobody's turned the lights on yet
and Richie shows up walking towards me he's in a spot-
light grinning from ear to ear and I know exactly what
he's going to do and all I have is this pencil, only a pencil
for gawd's sake
and he just keeps coming and he's laughing now and he
knows he's got me, he's smirking and walking
and I'm trembling and hating myself for trembling hating myself for being afraid for being scared shitless hating
my heart for slamming its way out of my chest my feet
nailed to the floor by Richie's grin and my own fear
and I pray
God help me
God please
please help me*

and I lift my left arm to push him back but my arm is shaking so bad I can hardly lift it up and Richie grabs my forearm and twists it down to my side and laughs and his tongue is curling out toward me long and vile like a thick ugly slug and I hate what's coming I hate him I hate being used and scared and dead inside and with my free right hand I slam the pencil into his eye

he just stands there
one bug-eye bulging
he is still grinning
his tongue dripping
saliva
twisting back
on itself
and I scream at him
*this is **my** dream*
***my** dream*
***my** dream*
and I shove the pencil in deeper harder farther
and he looks so surprised
with his one eye
and he collapses
stumbling off the stage
and over the edge and
lies in a heap looking
cheap and crumpled

and small and dead.
and I roll him over with the toe of my shoe and
bend down to touch him because as much as I dread it
I have to be sure absolutely certain beyond
any shadow of my dream that he will stay dead
and when I stand up again
I can breathe
walk away
But I know I will never sleep
like other people sleep
Deep.
Untroubled.

EPILOGUE

In 1963, no-one knew about Asperger's and my father didn't know I had been sexually abused, and to this day, I don't know what my mother thought. They had no cues to help them decode my rebellious and socially challenged behaviours. To them I was just a difficult child who at times could be charming and obedient, but who mostly exhibited unpredictable and often embarrassing behaviours.

This became especially prominent in my teens. While other teenagers wanted to be different, they only really wanted to be different from their parents, not their peer group. When it came to teen social circles, it was all about fitting in.

Not so for me. I wanted to be the one and only Margaret Jean on the planet, and I wanted to be indelibly stamped as that single original sample of humanity whose Margaret Jeanness would shine through everything she did and permeate every cell of her body. This intention often led to behaviour that resulted in ridicule or ostracism.

Asperger's Syndrome is a form of Autism that was first diagnosed in Austria by Dr. Hans Asperger in 1944. It wasn't until 1981 that a report by a Dr. Laura Wing brought more attention to the syndrome. I was still sixteen in the summer of 1963, almost two decades before Dr. Wing's report, and I do not recall my parents ever mentioning the term.

I was fifty years old when I received a phone call from my daughter, Bev, who had a special needs son who defied diagnosis. Almost from his birth, we would spend hours discussing Dustin's behaviours, and often noted that I could recall similar situations with his mother, and even sometimes in my own childhood. This particular day she called from their home on Vancouver Island. "Mom!" she exclaimed, "I finally know what Dustin has! And guess what? You and I also exhibit every single symptom!"

One by one she went through the checklist:

- Not pick up on social cues and may lack inborn social skills, such as being able to read others' body language, start or maintain a conversation, and take turns talking.
- Dislike any changes in routines.
- Appear to lack empathy.

- Be unable to recognize subtle differences in speech tone, pitch, and accent that alter the meaning of others' speech.
- Have a formal style of speaking that is advanced for his or her age.
- Avoid eye contact or stare at others.
- Have unusual facial expressions or postures.
- Be preoccupied with only one or few interests, which he or she may be very knowledgeable about.
- Talk a lot, usually about a favorite subject. One-sided conversations are common. Internal thoughts are often verbalized.
- ᶠHave heightened sensitivity and become over-stimulated by loud noises, lights, or strong tastes or textures.

After I hung up, I looked up the syndrome online. There was actually a conference on Asperger's scheduled in the next two weeks in our area. It was for education assistants, social workers, and other professionals who dealt with people with Asperger's. But Bev phoned and as a parent with a recently diagnosed child, she got permission to attend, and to bring me with her.

---

f   From Web MD Autism Spectrum Disorders Health Center, Asperger's Syndrome Symptoms.
http://www.webmd.com/brain/autism/tc/aspergers-syndrome-symptoms

I still vividly recall that conference, Bev and I sitting in the audience, tears flowing down my face. The presenter was describing my life, my anxieties, and my issues. I kept thinking of Roberta Flack's number one hit "Killing Me Softly" and the lines "Strumming my pain with his fingers", and "Telling my whole life with his words". That is how it felt to be there.

At times, Bev and I would laugh aloud (a fine example of inappropriate behaviour typical of people with Asperger's) and nudge each other as the speaker elaborated on "odd" behaviours so familiar to us. It was a joyous moment of shared recognition.

And one of grieving. Grieving for the loss of all those years, all that pain, all that disconnectedness. Grieving for having struggled all those years. Like a bird who is blind trying to fly out of a heavily treed forest, who constantly bashes into trunks and branches, wondering how all the other birds, calling him home from the tree tops, knew the way.

I'd like to say my life changed immediately but it didn't. It would take years for me to learn to connect to others in a way that was meaningful for them, years for me to move out of my self-centered focus and be able to look up at the people around me and see their needs as separate issues unrelated to mine. I never was perfect and I never will be, but I like to think that's not all Asperger's. I like to think at least some of it is just part of being a runner in the human race.

My family loved me, even if they couldn't understand me. They wouldn't let go. No matter how I behaved, or who I married, or how cloistered I lived, they kept coming back, drawing me in. For most of my life, I communicated from the outskirts of those relationships.

But over time, my sister and my daughters have matured into my best friends. They have all coached me on "normal behaviour" though they would never in a million years put it to me that way. Ironically, once I learned that Asperger's syndrome sufferers can't learn social behaviour from observation the way most children do, I began to make a point of observing and copying behaviours. Sometimes I still get it wrong, but I've learned a smile and a genuine interest in people goes a long way.

As a child in the little brown Baptist Church Sunday School, I learned things about God that I set aside. To do so cost me a great deal in terms of being able to build my life on a firm foundation within socially acceptable boundaries. I forgot the most important message, see? God loves you. You are perfect in his sight.

Post 1963:

Nick W. fell in love with a girl in college, and followed her to South America and married her. They both became professors at South American institutions.

Harold Banks was convicted in 1988 on 13 counts of sexual abuse and assault. On his arrest, police found notes on more than 1,000 incidents where he had abused or sexually interfered with children. He served his time and was released into the public. His last known address was in a small community on Vancouver Island.

Richie's life after Langford is unknown.

ENDNOTES

1 **Maria:** Tommy's "friend". With her husband & son, she rented the cabin on the Adam property after Mike and his family split up and went their separate ways. Maria separated from and then divorced her husband while living in the cabin. Come to think of it, everyone who lived in the cabin got divorced. Even the couple who moved their trailer onto our field, got divorced. On the other hand, Mom and Dad spent sixty-six years in the see-sawing dynamic of their marriage.

2 **Terry:** Margaret's younger sister by eight years, Terry is pretty and plump, with blonde hair down to her waist, which her father, Tommy, insists her mother, Edna keep in ringlets. The long hair gives the little girl headaches and the process of tying it up in rags to make it curl, is a time-consuming task

at the end of our mother's day of long hours and hard labour.

One night, in a stroke of inspiration, Mom takes the kitchen scissors and whacks off Terry's pony tail. My sister screams hysterically as Mom takes a bowl and fashions Terry's bangs into a neat even line above her brows.

My father comes home and sees with horror, the result. Gone are Terry's golden curls. He rants and raves and hollers, Terry's sobs a fitting accompaniment.

Eyeing them both as calmly as possible under the circumstances, Mom struggles to feel shame, but relief triumphs: with one stroke of the scissors, she has freed herself from the time-consuming nightly ritual of "putting up" Terry's hair in rags.

3   **Luke, Floyd and Tommy** are all brothers, sons of Jim and Esme Adam. Floyd, the oldest, Luke second and Tommy the sensitive "baby" of the boys.

Although he always cries at funerals and parades, he is still tougher than most men, including his violent father, now ten years dead. The family feels toward Tommy as the Old Testament people felt toward their God; we both feared and respected him, and whenever we could, we sought freedom from his tyranny.

4

5 **Steve: Floyd's** son, and thus Joe's nephew, who married Edna's sister, making Steve both cousin & uncle to Margaret Jean. A fine looking young man with a head of curly hair, gone prematurely grey, Steve, though much younger, became Tommy's drinking buddy and close companion.

6 **Kenny:** One of Edna's younger brothers, who also moved to B.C. A miner who at some point, worked with Margaret Jean's second husband, Edward, in the mines.

Once when she was visiting in their spotless mobile home, enjoying one of Aunt Helena's savoury butter tarts, she asked her uncle about environmental measures in the mining industry. Kenny grinned, then said: *"Unofficially? The company motto is: The best so-lution for po-llution is di-lution."* Kenny lived to the age of 76 when he died of a heart attack while running to put out a grass fire in his back yard.

7   **Terry** was visiting her cousins.

8   **Nell** is Tommy's sister, the youngest sibling and only girl. Esme cannot live with her daughter due to a severe personality clash. In many ways, Edna is more of daughter to Esme, but nevertheless, she is very fond of Nell. Nell is a practical nurse and nursed in the WREN Corps. Edna is a laborer in the sweaty confines of the Empress Laundry, and will later work cleaning motel rooms, and during the war, instead of heading to the armed forces for a glamorous career, she stayed home to help out Esme and Jim on the farm.

9   Margaret Jean called him **Nicholas** at times, but mostly Nick. It was astounding, half a century later to note that in Gram's mind, as illustrated in her diary, she thought of Margaret Jean's 6'2" ruggedly built boyfriend of German descent (remember, we were not long out of WWII) as "Nicky".

10 I am not sure if it was the Asperger's or just being a teenager, but I had no idea of the shape, size or geography of our Island, let alone the routes to anywhere. I could drive from one part of town to the other if I had been there before, but I had no concept of how the areas were geologically

connected. I remember being surprised to learn View Royal and the Gorge district were located on salt water bodies.

11 **Clark Boswell.** I met Clark in Oak Bay when I was 13 and he was 17 and we remained friends until I married. He was in college studying to be an accountant (what a catch!) and I had absolutely no romantic feelings for him whatsoever. Because I met him through Cheryl, a friend I made in Bible camp, my parents didn't scrutinize what I did when I spent the weekend with her. In fact, Cheryl and I spent time with boys like Clark, going to the movies, to jazz coffee houses, to the park or out for lunch. We would often go with a few of his friends from college, and the talk would center on art, literature and philosophy. Clark once told me he discussed some of my poetry with them, which amazed me then and still does now.

12 **The Devonshire Store.** All the way over on Peatt Road. How enlightened I must have felt, bypassing Coopers' and Price's stores to walk another four blocks to the Devonshire. How could I possibly have persuaded Grams that such frivolity was necessary?

13 **Cora:** One of Gram's sisters, who lived in San Diego, California and worked as a secretary at the San Diego Zoo.

14 **Zoonooz:** As Steve M. was Cora's husband, I can only assume this is the newsletter generated by the San Diego Zoo.

15 I can't really tell if Sawatsky, Ducovski and Ewaschuk were the same person, but I'm thinking they were.